Career Woman

The Violence of Modern Jobs

And The Lost Art of Home Making

By
Dr. Sahadeva dasa

B.com., FCA., AICWA., PhD
Chartered Accountant

Soul Science University Press
www.womenliberation.org

Readers interested in the subject matter of this
book are invited to correspond with the publisher at:
SoulScienceUniversity@gmail.com   +91 98490 95990
or visit DrDasa.com

First Edition: January 2015

Soul Science University Press expresses its gratitude to the
Bhaktivedanta Book Trust International (BBT), for the use of quotes by
His Divine Grace A.C.Bhaktivedanta Swami Prabhupada.

©Soul Science University Press
All rights reserved

ISBN 97893-82947-14-1

Published by:
Dr. Sahadeva dasa for Soul Science University Press

Printed by:
Rainbow Print Pack, Hyderabad

To order a copy write to purnabramhadasa@gmail.com
or buy online: Amazon.com, rlbdeshop.com

Dedicated to....

His Divine Grace A.C.Bhaktivedanta Swami Prabhupada

God has made women and man and they have got their respective duties. What women can do, man cannot do. What man can do women can not do.
How they can be equated? That is not possible. Everyone should do his own duty. They have women's liberation movement in America and they want equal opportunity for women.
But where is that liberation? The women has to carry the child for ten months. That is the Nature's way. Can the women transfer the responsibility of child birth to the man? As soon as the body is different how can there be equality?

~ Srila Prabhupada *(Letter to Ed Gilbert, 9 September, 1975)*

By The Same Author

Oil-Final Countdown To A Global Crisis And Its Solutions
End of Modern Civilization And Alternative Future
To Kill Cow Means To End Human Civilization
Cow And Humanity - Made For Each Other
Cows Are Cool - Love 'Em!
Let's Be Friends - A Curious, Calm Cow
Wondrous Glories of Vraja
We Feel Just Like You Do
Tsunami Of Diseases Headed Our Way - Know Your Food Before Time Runs Out
Cow Killing And Beef Export - The Master Plan To Turn India Into A Desert
Capitalism Communism And Cowism - A New Economics For The 21st Century
Noble Cow - Munching Grass, Looking Curious And Just Hanging Around
World - Through The Eyes Of Scriptures
To Save Time Is To Lengthen Life
Life Is Nothing But Time - Time Is Life, Life Is Time
Lost Time Is Never Found Again
Spare Us Some Carcasses - An Appeal From The Vultures
An Inch of Time Can Not Be Bought With A Mile of Gold
Cow Dung For Food Security And Survival of Human Race
Cow Dung – A Down To Earth Solution To Global Warming And Climate Change
Corporatocracy - You Are A Corporate Citizen, A Slave of Invisible And Ruthless Masters
Working Moms And The Rise of A Lost Generation
Glories of Thy Wondrous Name
India A World Leader in Cow Killing And Beef Export - An Italian Did It In 10 Years
As Long As There Are Slaughterhouses, There Will Be Wars
Peak Soil – Industrial Civilization, On The Verge of Eating Itself
If Violence Has To Stop, Slaughterhouses Must Close Down
(More information on availability on DrDasa.com)

Contents

Preface

1. Women Are More Unhappy
Despite 40 Years Of Feminism — 10
2. Women Can't Have It All
Indra Nooyi : PepsiCo Chairman And CEO — 14
3. Is A Woman's Place In The Home? — 20
4. Here's Absolute Proof
Mothers Are Better Off Staying At Home — 26
5. A Woman's Work Is Never Done
Burden of Two Full Time Jobs — 29
6. Working Mothers
Trapped By 'Double Burden' Of Guilt — 49
7. Stress Of A Career
Leading To Smoking And Drinking, Harming Women's Health — 52
8. Daily Juggling Acts Crippling Modern Women — 56
9. Modern India - Killing Its Urban Working Women — 58
10. Diabetes
More Common in Stressed Out, Working Women — 66
11. Working Women And Their Back Pain Woes — 68
12. Modern Slave Camps
Call Centre Workers Limited To
Eight Minutes Toilet Time Per Day — 72
13. Why Women Leave Tech
It's The Slavery, Not Because 'Math Is Hard' — 82
14. Soaring Number Of Career Women
'Killed By Alcohol' And Figure Is Rising Faster Than Men — 88
15. It Takes A Village To Raise A Child
No Mom Is an Island — 93

16 Why Women Still Can't Have It All	97
17 The Lost Art of Full-Time Homemaking	136
18 They Wear Nappies, Drink Cola And Don't Know How To Open A Book. One Teacher's Terrifying Insight Into 5-Year-Olds Failed By Their Parents	141
19 Too Busy To Potty Train Your Child? Meet The Experts Who Say They Can Get The Job Done In Just Two Days - For $1,750	153
20 Married Couples' Health Suffers When Men Earn Less Than Wives	156
21 Women Should Do All the Housework To Avoid Divorce Study Suggests	158
22 Wives Really Are The Glue That Hold Marriages Together Those Who Calm Down Quickly After Arguments Have The Best Relationships	161
23 Adopting The Fifties Lifestyle To Save Their Marriages	165
24 Happy Wife Makes Happy Marriages	170
25 The Power of Less The Fine Art of Limiting Yourself to the Essential....In Business And In Life	173
26 Slow Movements	177
27 Why Giving Up Your Job Could Be Your Best Career Move Ever!	187
28 Three Tons Of Food Per Year From A 1/10 Acre City Lot	194
29 Need For A Social Structure	197

The Author

Preface

A civilization, in order to survive, must be successfully transmitted from one generation to the next. Woman plays the most important role in this transmission. She is the first teacher of the child. In that sense, women have always provided the foundational support for civilization. The edifice of our modern society would never have existed if not for the civilizing influence of women upon men.

According to Alpin MacLaren, Women cause men to settle down, and to look to family and security. Women inspire men to achieve in the business world by their moral support and yes, their need to be provided for. Women have trained the boys of each generation to behave in a civilized society. The traditional role women have had in civilization is critical and provides the foundation for everything else.

Now, remove that influence and what happens? Look around you and there you will see the answer. According to MacLaren, feminism has pulled the foundation out from under our civilization, by convincing women that in the workforce lies their destiny instead of being wives and mothers. Men are now forced to compete with women at work instead of joining with them in a family. The house where couples live is no longer a home, where children are always cared for and supervised. Men are no longer in a position of sole bread winner and therefore do not have a known and well defined role in the family. They are leaving their families in record numbers every day. Civilization is beginning to crumble rapidly, as crime increases and neighborhoods become nothing but a collection of strangers who do not take care of each other. Children are raising themselves and learning many things from their friends, television, movies and even the internet, that parents should be appalled at. But since the foundation of our society has been removed, the trend of the "work-orphaned" children continues and accelerates.

Gita warned us about this long ago: When irreligion is prominent in the family, O Krsna, the women of the family become polluted, and from the degradation of womanhood, O descendant of Vrsni, comes unwanted progeny (Bg 1.40). By the evil deeds of those who destroy the family tradition and thus give rise to unwanted children, all kinds of community projects and family welfare activities are devastated (Bg 1.42).

Somewhere in the struggle for gender equity, woman lost her happiness. In The Paradox of Declining Female Happiness, Betsey Stevenson and Justin Wolfers of the University of Pennsylvania, begin by noting the gains.

"By many measures the progress of women over recent decades has been extraordinary: the gender wage gap has partly closed; educational attainment has risen and is now surpassing that of men; women have gained an unprecedented level of control over fertility; (and) technological change in the form of new domestic appliances has freed women from domestic drudgery."

Yet Stevenson and Wolfers have found that in America women's happiness, far from rising, has fallen "both absolutely and relatively to that of men". Where women in the 1970s reported themselves to be significantly happier than men, now for the first time they are reporting levels of happiness lower than men.

The authors readily admit that measuring happiness is necessarily a subjective task, but the overall trend from the data, compiled from social surveys conducted over many years, is "clear and compelling".

Sahadeva dasa

Dr. Sahadeva dasa
31st January 2015
Secunderabad, India

1

Women Are More Unhappy

Despite 40 Years Of Feminism

Claims Study

Women are less happy nowadays despite 40 years of feminism, a new study claims.

Despite having more opportunities than ever before, they have a lower sense of well-being and life satisfaction, it found.

The study, The Paradox of Declining Female Happiness, said the same was true for women of different ages and whether or not they were married or had children.

It said the results appeared surprising given that modern women had been liberated from their traditional 1950s role of housewife.

Instead, their earning power has soared, women are doing better than men in education and they are in control of decisions over whether to start a family.

The study by the US National Bureau of Economic Research found that while post-war era happiness surveys found women were noticeable happier than men, the difference had eroded to 'zero'.

Its authors, Betsey Stevenson and Justin Wolfers of the University of Pennsylvania, found that in the U.S., women's happiness had fallen 'both absolutely and relatively to that of men'.

In 12 European countries the happiness of women has fallen relative to that of men.

Siobhan Freegard, founder of the website Netmums, whose own survey found levels of 'baby blues' have risen sharply compared to 30 years ago, said: 'We pushed so hard for equal rights, for having the right to work, for having equal status, we pushed so hard to have choice.

'But what we hear from many mums is: I have no choice, I have to work, I don't love my career, my childminder is taking half my salary and I'd rather bring up my children myself but I can't afford to.

'If you enjoy your job and it's a fulfilling career, that is a positive choice.. but if it's not, it's almost in some ways that we got it all, then found that actually it wasn't quite what we wanted.'

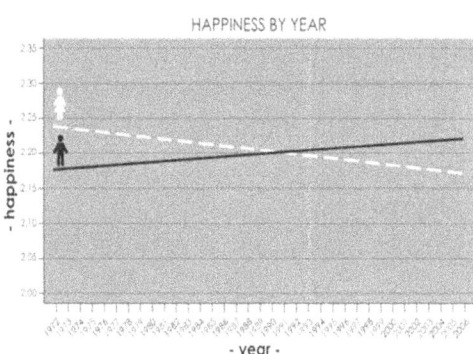

Erin Pizzey, founder of the charity Refuge, added: 'The hard-won freedom of choice has imprisoned women. I just see an exhausted generation trying to do it all.'

And, in case you're wondering, this finding is neither unique to this one study, nor is it unique to one country. In the last couple of years, the results from six major studies of happiness have been released:

* the United States General Social Survey (46,000 people, between 1972-2007),
* the Virginia Slims Survey of American Women (26,000 people, between 1972-2000),
* the Monitoring the Future survey (430,000 U.S. twelfth graders, between 1976-2005),
* the British Household Panel Study (121,000 people, between 1991-2004),
* the Eurobarometer analysis (636,000 people, between 1973-2002, covering fifteen countries),
* and the International Social Survey Program (97,462 people, between 1991-2001, covering thirty-five developed countries.)

All told, more than 1.3 million men and women have been surveyed over the last 40 years, both here in the U.S. and in developed countries around the world. Wherever researchers have been able to collect reliable data on happiness, the finding is always the same: greater educational, political, and employment opportunities have corresponded to decreases in life happiness for women, as compared to men.

> *Ms. Nixon: How do you feel about women's liberation?*
> *Srila Prabhupada: So-called equal rights for women means that the men cheat the women. Suppose a woman and a man meet, they become lovers, they have sex, the woman becomes pregnant, and the man goes away. The woman has to take charge of the child and beg alms from the government, or else she kills the child by having an abortion. This is the woman's independence. In India, although a woman may be poverty-stricken, she stays under the care of her husband, and he takes responsibility for her. When she becomes pregnant, she is not forced to kill the child or maintain him by begging. So, which is real independence -- to remain under the care of the husband or to be enjoyed by everyone?*
> *~ Srila Prabhupada (Science of Self-realization)*

Career Woman - The Violence of Modern Jobs And The Lost Art of Home Making

Source:

Olinka Koster, The Daily Mail, 1 June 2009

Marcus Buckingham, Find Your Strongest Life: What the Happiest and Most Successful Women Do Differently

Bloomberg Business Week, October 16, 2009

Marcus Buckingham, The Huffington Post, 17/11/2009

Happy or Right? The Modern Day Woman's Dilemma, Sara Plummer, Apr 27, 2013

2

Women Can't Have It All

Indra Nooyi : PepsiCo Chairman And CEO

Chief says she 'dies with guilt' over compromises she makes to balance career and family life

With her stellar career, £7.3million salary, 34-year marriage and two much-loved children, there doesn't seem to be much missing from Indra Nooyi's life.

But despite appearances, the CEO of PepsiCo insists that women can't have it all – and can only 'pretend' to.

Mrs Nooyi, who is ranked at number 13 on this year's Forbes list of the world's most powerful women, says she has sacrificed relationships to get ahead at work and 'dies with guilt' over the compromises she makes to balance her career with her family life.

The 58-year-old even described enlisting her secretary to control how much time her daughters spent playing video games.

On Whether Women Can "Have It All"

'I don't think women can have it all. I just don't think so. We pretend we have it all. We pretend we can have it all. My husband and I have been married for 34 years. And we have two daughters. And every day you have to make a decision about whether you are going to be a wife or a mother, in fact many times during the day you have to make those decisions. And you have to co-opt a lot of

Career Woman - The Violence of Modern Jobs And The Lost Art of Home Making

'Women can't have it all': Indra Nooyi, CEO of PepsiCo, told those gathered at Aspen Ideas Festival that it is nearly impossible for women to balance work and family without help

people to help you. We co-opted our families to help us. We plan our lives meticulously so we can be decent parents. But if you ask our daughters, I'm not sure they will say that I've been a good mom. I'm not sure. And I try all kinds of coping mechanisms. 'You know, you have to cope, because you die with guilt.'

Her comments echo those of Facebook CEO and mother-of-two Sheryl Sandberg, who said earlier this year that there is no such thing as a work-life balance, adding: 'There's work, and there's life, and there's no balance.'

At the Aspen Ideas Festival in Colorado, Mrs Nooyi, who studied business at Yale University, also suggested a woman's 'biological clock and career clock are in total, complete conflict with each other'.

On Starting A Family

My observation…is that the biological clock and the career clock are in total conflict with each other. Total, complete conflict. When you have to have kids you have to build your career. Just as you're rising to middle management your kids need you because they're teenagers, they need you for the teenage years.

And that's the time your husband becomes a teenager too, so he needs you. They need you too. What do you do? And as you grow even more, your parents need you because they're aging.

So we're screwed.

'The person who hurts the most through this whole thing is your spouse. There's no question about it. You know, [my husband] Raj always said, you know what, your list is PepsiCo, PepsiCo, PepsiCo, our two kids, your mom, and then at the bottom of the list is me.'

> I'll tell you a story that happened when my daughter went to Catholic school. Every Wednesday morning they had class coffee with the mothers. Class coffee for a working woman—how is it going to work? How am I going to take off 9 o'clock on Wednesday mornings? So I missed most class coffees. My daughter would come home and she would list off all the mothers that were there and say, "You were not there, mom."
>
> The first few times I would die with guilt. But I developed coping mechanisms. I called the school and I said, "give me a list of mothers that are not there." So when she came home in the evening she said, "You were not there, you were not there."
>
> And I said, "ah ha, Mrs. Redd wasn't there, Mrs. So and So wasn't there. So I'm not the only bad mother."
>
> You know, you have to cope, because you die with guilt. You just die with guilt. My observation is that the biological clock and the career clock are in total conflict with each other. Total, complete conflict. When you have to have kids you have to build your career. Just as you're rising to middle management your kids need you because they're teenagers, they need you for the teenage years.
>
> ~ Indra Nooyi, At the Aspen Ideas Festival in Colorado

Career Woman - The Violence of Modern Jobs And The Lost Art of Home Making

Family life: Indra poses with her husband Raj and their two daughters

She joked: 'There are two ways to look at it. You should be happy you're on the list. So don't complain. He is on the list. He is very much on the list.'

Mrs Nooyi also described how she needed to outsource parenting tasks to her receptionist to make sure her daughters did not spend too much time playing video games.

She said: 'I travel a lot, and when my kids were tiny, especially my second one, we had strict rules on playing Nintendo. She'd call the office, and she didn't care if I was in China, Japan, India, wherever.'

The Pepsi boss said she gave her secretary a list of questions to ask her daughter before she could have permission to play the games.

> *Now let us cooperate. In New Vrindaban the women's business will be to take care of the children, to cook, to clean and to churn butter, and, for those who have the knowledge, to help in typing. No other hard work -- that's all. But for the men, there is hard work -- working in the field, taking care of the animals, collecting food, constructing buildings. So in this way we should cooperate.*
>
> ~ Srila Prabhupada (Lecture, West Virginia, May 23, 1972)

She explained: 'She goes through the questions and she says, "Okay, you can play Nintendo half an hour." Then she leaves me a message. "Tyra called at five. This is the sequence of questions I went through. I've given her permission." So it's seamless parenting.

> Q. You come home one day as president of the company, just appointed, and your mom is not that impressed. Would you tell that story?
> Indira: This is about 14 years ago. I was working in the office. I work very late, and we were in the middle of the Quaker Oats acquisition. And I got a call about 9:30 in the night from the existing chairman and CEO at that time. He said, Indra, we're going to announce you as president and put you on the board of directors... I was overwhelmed, because look at my background and where I came from—to be president of an iconic American company and to be on the board of directors, I thought something special had happened to me.
> So rather than stay and work until midnight which I normally would've done because I had so much work to do, I decided to go home and share the good news with my family. I got home about 10, got into the garage, and my mother was waiting at the top of the stairs. And I said, "Mom, I've got great news for you." She said, "let the news wait. Can you go out and get some milk?" I looked in the garage and it looked like my husband was home. I said, "what time did he get home?" She said "8 o'clock." I said, "Why didn't you ask him to buy the milk?" "He's tired." Okay. We have a couple of help at home, "why didn't you ask them to get the milk?" She said, "I forgot." She said just get the milk. We need it for the morning. So like a dutiful daughter, I went out and got the milk and came back.
> I banged it on the counter and I said, "I had great news for you. I've just been told that I'm going to be president on the Board of Directors. And all that you want me to do is go out and get the milk, what kind of a mom are you?" And she said to me, "let me explain something to you. You might be president of PepsiCo. You might be on the board of directors. But when you enter this house, you're the wife, you're the daughter, you're the daughter-in-law, you're the mother. You're all of that. Nobody else can take that place. So leave that damned crown in the garage. And don't bring it into the house.
> ~ Indra Nooyi, At the Aspen Ideas Festival in Colorado

On Juggling Career And Family

'Train people at work. Train your family to be your extended family.... If you don't develop mechanisms with your secretaries, with the extended office, with everybody around you, it cannot work. You know, stay at home mothering was a full time job. Being a CEO for a company is three full time jobs rolled into one. How can you do justice to all? You can't.'

Source
Emily Davies, Daily Mail, 3 July 2014
Conor Friedersdorf, The Atlantic, July 1, 2014
Amna Nawaz, NBC News, 2 Jul 2014
Drake Baer, Business Insider, Oct 31, 2014

Artificially... Suppose a woman is trying to become man artificially, how long it will go on? How she can be happy? That is not possible. Actually, in the Western countries at least we see that the woman class, they want equal rights with men. And there is. There is no distinction. But it is my experience, the woman class, they are not happy in the Western countries. And still in our country, although we are so fallen, still our woman class remains satisfied. Being predominated, they are happy. They are happy. That is my practical experience.

~ Srila Prabhupada (Bhagavad-gita Lecture -- Ahmedabad, December 8, 1972)

3

Is A Woman's Place In The Home?

By Glynis Hay Rickards

I glanced at my watch; it was 3:30 p.m. I logged off the computer picked up my car keys and signaled to my boss. He knows the meaning of that familiar signal. It means I am dashing off to pick up my kids (ages 10 and 13) from school. After picking them up I will take them home and leave them to perform the familiar routine that they have been practicing for years.

First they will have their bath, then take the microwave able containers with the specific day labeled from the fridge, placed it in the microwave oven, have their dinner, complete their assignments and then head to the baby sitter. The baby sitter being none other than the good old television set or their video games. I would call from my office occasionally to ensure that everything is okay. They have strict orders not to open doors to strangers, and all emergency numbers are at their fingertips. This routine has taught them to be responsible and independent children.

At approximately 7:00 pm I would drag myself home, check their assignments, have a little chit-chat with them and then head off to bed.

Good Old Days

I compared this to the days when I used to get the bus home from school and would be greeted by my mother with a smile on her face and a cool drink in her hand. She would ask us the familiar question, which we sometimes forget to answer. "How was school today? Did you enjoy you nice lunch that I packed in your lunch kit"? After our bath we would sit at the dining table and enjoy a nice warm meal while sharing the days events.

In retrospect I can only ask myself this question. "What has happened to those good old days"? Why did women abandon their place in the home?

Why Did Women Abandon Their Place In The Home?

Prior to the Industrial Revolution which took place in the Eighteenth Century there was no place for women in the work world because most tasks required manual labour and therefore women would not be considered for such tasks because physical strength was required for effective performance.

The advent of the Industrial Revolution, which can be described as the historical transformation of traditional into modern societies, saw the birth of mechanization for manufacturing and other processes. Machines were invented to perform most jobs and the need for women to operate these machines became apparent. Piece work shops and textile factories along with other factories were established and women became a part of the workforce.

It was noted that most women joined the work force out of economic necessity. The ability to earn wages provided them with a better standard of living, independence, and mobility, and also self esteem, since they were now able to contribute to the world's economic development.

While they enjoyed the status of being independent they had to deal with the negative aspects of being a woman in the working world. Women were forced to deal with the lack of amenities. For example proper rest rooms were not available.

Their home life suffered because they had to deal with working a full day in the factory then returning home to perform their domestic chores and looking after their family. They would sometimes perform similar jobs to men but would receive less wages and also had to deal with the pressures of sexual harassment. Women received high praises for their performance on the job, but they were deprived of promotional opportunities and rewards because of their gender.

"Darling, what's happened to us?"

Despite strides towards gender equality women are still being victimized and denied promotions because they are seen as "not tough enough" for the position. A survey done by the International Labor Organization revealed that women's overall share of management jobs rarely exceeds twenty per cent. There have also been litigations and various organizations have been established with the main aim being to end institutionalized discrimination against women.

> *The man and woman in your country, they have got equal rights. Why not here? (laughter) In the lavatory? Why this discrimination, "woman," "man," why? Equal rights, must be equal rights.*
> ~ Srila Prabhupada (Morning Walk -- May 4, 1973, Los Angeles)

Absence of Mother - Development Of Mistrust In The Child

The process of socialization can be negatively affected by the absence of women in the home. While men are seen as the head of the family the women are often responsible for providing the foundation for primary socialization to take place. "Socialization is the process by which individuals learn the culture of their society". (Haralambos, 1990, p. 4).

Primary socialization is the most important factor of the socialization process as this takes place during infancy. During this process, which can be described as a "getting to know you" period, the child develops a bond with the family. The child copies the behaviour of the parents, respond to the approval and disapproval of the parents and also learns the language and develops social etiquette. While the father helps in this process the mother is instrumental because of the natural bond which exist between mother and child.

Psychoanalysis (Erikson, 1973) research on psychosocial development proved that; "During the oral-sensory stage which is between birth and eighteen months, the basic crisis centers around the development of either trust or mistrust". A child is completely dependent on others for the fulfillment of his needs e.g. feeding. If these needs are consistently satisfied and if he receives love and stimulation he will develop a sense of trust, not only in others but also in himself.

If, on the other hand, his needs are not satisfied regularly and he receives little love, attention and stimulation, he will develop a sense of mistrust. The presence of the mother at this stage of development is important because of the mother child relationship and it is therefore easier for the mother to successful guide the child through this stage of development.

Deterioration of Family Values

The deterioration of family norms and values has been attributed to the absence of women in the home. When a child enters society they must learn specific guidelines, which determines acceptable and appropriate behaviour within a culture or society. In short they must learn what is right and what is wrong. These "rights and wrongs" are the norms of a society. The child would be taught general social conducts i.e. appropriate and inappropriate behaviour. Again the mother is normally the chief individual who ensures that these norms are upheld and failure to do so would result in the use of positive of negative sanctions, which are actually rewards and punishment.

Pusta Krsna: There was an article in the newspaper about that today. Very interesting. It said in the newspaper that if women stop breast feeding their children they will have to increase the population of dairy cows tremendously. A very small percentage do now.

Prabhupada: They have to increase?

Pusta Krsna: More and more cows to produce enough milk to feed children.

Prabhupada: And therefore we are killing children. There is no problem, we shall kill our.... Let us kill, wholesale. And go to ball dance.

Hari-sauri: The whole civilization is completely crazy.

Prabhupada: Kartikeya told me. After many years he went to see his mother, and mother was going to ball dance. And mother said, "Wait, I am coming back." And he was surprised. He told me. Son has come home after many years, and she could not talk with him. She was going to ball dance.

Pusta Krsna: It actually is that way. It actually goes on that way.

Prabhupada: This is the mother.

Hari-sauri: Completely callous.

Rupanuga: Not even motherly love anymore.

Prabhupada: Mother killing. He was about to be killed. He admits. His grandmother advised the mother. Mother advising young daughter to kill her child in the womb.

~ Srila Prabhupada (Room Conversation, July 4, 1976, Washington D.C.)

Values on the other hand are beliefs that there are thing, which are good and desirable and worthwhile striving to achieve. Values can be compared to materialistic achievements, thought it appears materialistic it also takes on the disguise of ambition and self confidence. For example aiming to be first in your class, being a doctor or a lawyer. These are all values that are instilled in us because we are a part of a family, and we are taught that the accumulation of material possession is a symbol to determine ones' achievement.

The birth of Generation X has been blamed on the absence of the mother in the home to provide continuous inspiration. The group of people born between 1961 and 1981 who are now viewed by society as having little hope for the future because they lack values and suffer from the lack of vision to need to achieve success.

Should women search for their aprons and cook spoons and reclaim their rightful place in the home? Or continue wearing linen suits and step boldly in leather high heels? Can women effectively contribute to society by playing the double role of homemaker and executive?

References
Anderson, M., Introduction to Erik Erikson's 8 Stages.
http://snycorva.cortland.edu/~ANDERSMD/ERIK/stageint.HTML (2001, January 27)
Creswell, Julie, & Bass, Dina (1998, December). The 50 Most Powerful Women in American
Business. Fortune 500 pp. 76 – 82.
Fanovich, Souzanne. (1998) . Introduction to Sociology. Barbados: University of the West
Indies Press (Original work published 1978).
Haralambos, M, & Holborn, M. (1991). Sociology Themes and Perspectives. London: HarperCollins.
Wirth, Linda. (1998) . Women in Management. Will the Glass Ceiling Ever be Broken.
World of Work: The Magazine of International Labor Organization.
http://www.ilo.org/public/english/bureau/inf/magazine/23/glass.htm (2001, February 1)

4

Here's Absolute Proof

Mothers Are Better Off Staying At Home

In our increasingly mad and dogma-driven world, most political slogans mean the opposite of what they seem to say. The best example of this is the phrase 'family-friendly'. This describes measures to ensure that most parents hardly ever see their children, who are instead brought up by paid strangers.

One 'family-friendly' policy is taxpayer subsidies for the network of day orphanages where abandoned children are detained without trial for long hours, while their mothers are chained to desks miles away.

Yes, we're laying it on a bit thick here, but nothing like as much as our opponents, who claim that mothers who stay at home to raise their own children are 'chained to the kitchen sink'.

"You'll have to excuse the mess... I have a working husband."

Career Woman - The Violence of Modern Jobs And The Lost Art of Home Making

This stupid expression is at the heart of a long and furious propaganda campaign against real family life, waged by weirdo revolutionaries since the 1960s. Originally doomed to failure, it suddenly succeeded when big business realised that female staff were cheaper and more reliable than men.

But our near-totalitarian propaganda machine, which pushes its views in school PSHE classes, TV and radio soap operas and countless advice columns, has succeeded brilliantly in making young mothers feel ashamed of being at home with their small children.

And here is the absolute proof of that. A significant number of homes – four per cent – lose money by having both parents at work. Many – ten per cent – gain nothing from this arrangement. Yet they still do it. Many more gain so little that it is barely worth the bother.

The most amazing statistic of the past year (produced by insurance company Aviva) shows that thousands of mothers who go out to work are, in effect, working for nothing. The cost of day orphanages, travel and other work expenses cancels out everything they earn.

Thousands of mothers who go out to work are, in effect, working for nothing, writes Peter Hitchens

Many more barely make a profit on the arrangement. One in four families has a parent who brings home less than £100 a month after all the costs of work have been met.

How strange. When people ignore their own material best interests, it is a clear sign that they have been deluded by propaganda or fashion, or both.

How much better it would be for everyone involved if these mothers stayed with their children. Both generations would be immensely happier, the children would be better brought-up, neighbourhoods, often deserted by day, would revive. Yet, because of a cynical alliance between Germaine Greer and the Fat Cats of the Corporations, and because almost all women in politics are furious believers in nationalised childhood, we spurn this wise policy, even if it costs us money.

Source
By Peter Hitchens, For The Mail On Sunday, 4 January 2015

> *One American woman, was.... She was speaking that "In India the woman are treated as slave. We don't want." So I told her that it is better to become slave of one person than to become slave of hundreds.*
> *~ Srila Prabhupada, Morning Walk, March 19, 1976, Mayapur, India*

5

A Woman's Work Is Never Done

Burden of Two Full Time Jobs

Double burden is a term describing the workload of women who work to earn money, but also have responsibility for unpaid, domestic labor. This phenomenon is also known as the "The Second Shift" as in Arlie Hochschild's book of the same name. In heterosexual couples where both partners have paid jobs, women often spend significantly more time on household chores and caring work, such as childrearing or caring for the sick, than men.

Due to an increase in the number of women participating in the labor market, efforts have been made document the effects of this double burden on couples placed in such situations. Many studies have been done tracing the effects of the gendered division of labor and in most cases there was a notable difference between the time men and women contribute to unpaid labor.

The term double burden arises from the fact that many men and women currently are responsible for both domestic labor and paid labor. However, due to the thinking that a woman's time spent in domestic work is more valuable than a woman's time spent doing paid work, and that a man's time spent doing paid work is more valuable than a man's time spent doing domestic work, there is the issue of women having to do a large amount of both paid and unpaid work, leading to the double burden. Some alternative terms for double burden include : double day, second shift, and double duty.

Many studies have been done to investigate the division of household labor within couples, and more specifically, on the gender roles played by a variety of people worldwide.

According to The State of the World's Children 2007, women generally work longer hours than men regardless if they live in a developed or developing country. Most studies found that when both parents are faced with a full-time job, women are faced with a higher amount of a domestic workload than men.

According to the World Bank Latin American and Caribbean Studies, Mexican women in the labor force still spend approximately 33 hours each week performing household responsibilities. In contrast, husbands only contribute approximately 6 hours each week. Even more striking, "daughters contribute 14 hours weekly helping

their mothers, while sons spend the same time as their fathers (that is, 5–6 hours weekly)."

In a study done by Statistics Canada's General Social Survey of 10,000 households, the average man spent under two hours a day dealing with childcare and house work while women on average spent a little more than three. This study highlights the unequal distribution of labor between partners. Of the people surveyed, under fifteen percent of the couples agreed on doing around the same amount of work in the house. About 83 percent of women participated in housecleaning and food preparation compared to only 51 percent of men who were surveyed.

'It's nearly midnight – could you finish the housework in the morning?'

John Frederick Conway's book, The Canadian Family in Crisis, explores effects of the double burden by gender. In Conway's studies, he discovers the physical, emotional, and psychological differences between men and women faced with the double burden in Canada. In these studies it was found that women who are raising children and are in the workforce are more prone to have anxiety and many other stress related effects than the women who are just faced with one of the two burdens.

Unequal Work Burdens Around The World - In The Industrialized World

Pre-World War II

The traditional female homemaker-male breadwinner model characterized female employment prior to World War II. At the turn of the 20th century in the United States "only 18 percent of women over the age of 13 participated in the labor force." These women were typically young, single, white, and native-born. In contrast, married women in the labor force were "predominantly blacks or immigrants and very poor." Working mothers often exited the labor force once their children were old enough to earn money.

The outpouring of occupational opportunities in the early 1920s, such as in "cafeterias, nurseries, laundries and other facilities seemed to release women from domestic chores and freed them to participate fully in the sphere of production." This migration of women into the workforce shook the traditional ideology of gender roles, but importantly, it was the catalyst to the double burden becoming noticeable.

The 1930s "encouraged women to fulfill what Stalin termed the "great and honorable duty that nature has given" them. Evident in the Soviet Union, "an officially sponsored cult of motherhood, buttressed by anti-abortion legislation" accompanied by a "depression of living standards" led to industry's immense demand for laborers which got women into the industrial workforce in unprecedented numbers."

Urban women thus found themselves assuming the "double burden" (also known as the "double shift") of waged work outside the home and the lion's share of unpaid labor within it." The Second World War is typically seen as a catalyst for increasing female employment. Best exemplified by Rosie the Riveter propaganda of an efficient, patriotic, woman worker, World War II increased demand for female labor to replace that of the "16 million men mobilized to serve in the Armed Forces".

While a substantial number of women worked in war factories, the majority of jobs were in the service sector. This caused the gendered expectations for that time to be altered and roles to be both tested and reassigned for the incoming decades.

Post-World War II

The post-World War II period is marked by relatively high levels of female participation in the workforce, particularly in industrialized countries. Although a large proportion of women exited the workforce immediately following World War II, the idea of working class women was able to take root and normalize.

"In 2001, 47 percent of U.S. workers were women, and 61 percent of women over the age of 15 were in the labor force." Besides an increased demand for women's labor, other factors contributed to the growth of their participation, such as more educational opportunities and later marriage and childbearing ages. The idea of the double burden fruther evolved with the times concerning both sexes and their newfound roles.

The role of a provider and caregiver is sometimes expected of women, but as more women enter the workforce, an 'independent' ideology seems to take effect and forces some women to decide between a career and family. Some may choose strictly one or the other, others may choose to carry the burden of both lifestyles.

Some "modern men tend to believe in the principle of equal sharing of domestic labor, but fail to actually live up to that belief." The constant tug of war regarding one's time and where it could,

Eastern Europe
Under socialism, everyone was guaranteed employment. However, women suffered the double burden of paid and unpaid work, leading to lower birth rates. The commitment to social equality and the issue of declining birth rates allowed women to have some rights, such as child care and child allowances. For example, in the Soviet Union, maternity leave was extended to three years and part-time work was introduced. With the collapse of communism, many of these rights have been revoked due to the new largely male oriented democracy that has been put in place. Although there has been an increase in female workers, their need for welfare support such as child care has not been met, and has been ignored.

should but will be spent creates a new speed bump that is a little bit higher than the previous ones.

Modern times illuminate the dilemma that many dual-income couples face when trying to reconcile unpaid domestic work and paid employment. The burden of encompassing both ideologies plays a toll on both sexes in today's societies.

Causes Of The Double Burden

Gender Ideology

Traditional gender ideologies have contributed to the double burden because it posits women as caretakers, men as providers, and each gender occupying their own sphere of influence. Although research has shown that attitudes about gender roles have become more egalitarian over the past few decades, "these changes in gender attitudes have not been accompanied by corresponding changes in the allocation of housework".

Labor Market Constraints

Despite women's increasing participation in the work force, a gender division of labor persist. There are a number of constraints in the labor market that contribute to the double burden. "Women are disproportionately represented in informal work and concentrated among lower-quality jobs within self-employment."

The informal market is generally precarious and characterized by low wages, few benefits, and a lack of social protections that are offered in the formal market.

There is dearth of women in senior or managerial positions due to institutional barriers and norms. Even in female-

A WOMAN'S WORK IS NEVER DONE

The extra hours women spend on unpaid duties around the home compared to men

Italy	21 hrs
Spain	15 hrs
UK	11 hrs
OECD average	10.5 hrs
USA	9 hrs
China	8 hrs
Poland	7 hrs
Slovenia	6 hrs
Belgium	5 hrs
Denmark	3 hrs

Source: OECD

dominated occupations, men often occupy the more skilled and better paid positions.

The gender wage gap is a possible consequence of occupational segregation. The gender wage gap is the "difference between wages earned by women and men". In 2008, globally, men were estimated to earn 16.5 per cent more than women.

Unfair Policies

It is also often common to think that women make economic decisions similarly to men. This is typically not the case, because for men, payment is simply a compensation for lost leisure time.

However, for women, when they are working in the paid sector, they are still losing money because they have to make provisions for the domestic labor they are unable to do, such as caring for children or making dinner from scratch due to lack of resources such as child care. Her net financial gain is less than the financial gain of a man because she has to spend her earnings on providing for these provisions.

In addition, increasing paid work hours in order to have more money may have negative effects on the woman due to the increased total work hours and decreased leisure time.

Therefore, policies that give greater power to people who do paid labor have an adverse effect on female employment and the effect that the double burden has on females. Such policies give greater power and consideration towards people who work in the paid sector, and less towards people who work in the unpaid sector.

You see here that all young girls are carrying water, collecting. In the morning collecting water, cleansing the house, utensils, clothes, taking bath, then cooking, those girls. Their first business. Man's business is to earn money, go to the market, the necessities. Woman's business is take care of household affairs, children, and they have got engagement.
(-Srila Prabhupada, Room Conversation, June 28, 1977, Vrindavan)

Occupational Segregation

Another political issue surrounding the double burden is what sort of policies directly or indirectly affect those who do domestic work. Some policies that companies have, such as a lower rate for part-time workers or firing workers when they get pregnant can be seen as disempowering women.

Debate as to whether this is gender segregation continues. On one side, only women get pregnant and there is a disproportionate amount of women who do part-time work instead of full-time, suggesting that there should be allowances made for women.

Increased Nuclearization Of Family

Due to the increasing trend of decreased fertility rate, there has been an increased nuclearization of the family, where families have less immediate relatives to depend on in times of need. Because of this phenomenon, families do not have an extended family to depend on when they need a caretaker or someone to do domestic work, and must turn to  market substitutes or a member of the immediate family doing both domestic and paid work instead.

Types Of Double Burdens

Work Vs. Family

Parenting is a large task within itself, and when a parent has a career as well, it can cause a double burden, or work–family conflict. Strain begins to develop when women and men find that the demands of their family are conflicting with the demands from their job. When one is faced with a double burden like this, it affects how decisions are made within a career and in a family; this burden could potentially effect when a couple decides to have children.

75% of all women who have jobs are in their childbearing prime. When the conflict between one's family and work presents itself, the unpaid work that is being done in the home may be cut down, because of the certain health effects, or as a solution to deal with the greater demands from the workplace.

Social outings and visits, and family dinners are two of the first things that get cut back on due to the work/family conflict. In a study by Ari Vananen, May V. Kevin, et al. found that if a man put a higher importance on their family, were more likely to stay home from work in order to deal with extreme family demands.

Ways that the double burden can be lessened for is with hired help in the house, day-care facilities, and longer maternity leaves for women. For instance, in Norway women are allowed the options of 10 months of maternity leave, where they will get 100% of their pay, or 12 months leave, where they will only paid 80% of their earnings.

Some companies are realizing the effect the double burden of work and a family is having on their employees and are offering flexible work schedules in order to help their employees cope. Not only do these flexible hours help the employee deal with their stress, but it also benefits the company because workers are happier, less

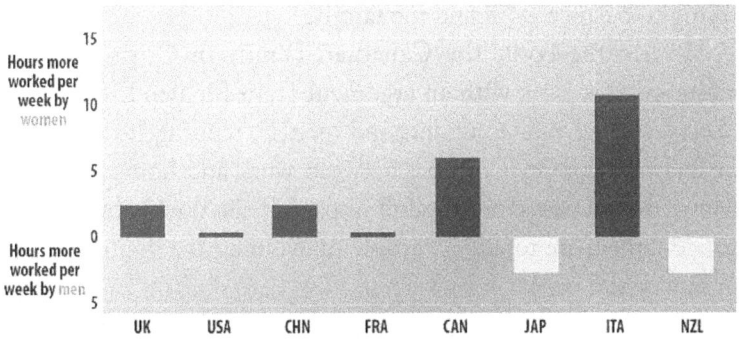

likely to be absent, more productive, and the turnover rate is lower for the company.

Family Vs. School

Raising a family is not an easy task, and deciding to go back to school while raising a family can be a monumental decision for the family. Some parents postpone pursuing higher education until their children are older, because they don't want to leave them in the hand of a baby sitter constantly at such a young age. However, once the children get older, the parent pursuing an education may start missing important events in their children's life.

Most of the time this burden will include the person trying to balance a job along with their family and schooling. Upgrading knowledge base has become essential and financial stability requires keeping up with the changing technologies.

Single Vs. Married Parents

Single Parent

Single Parents do not typically have the luxury of dividing tasks between two adults in the home. Married parents have that option to split the workload, even though it usually does not happen, but single parents do not have the option of sharing the workload with anyone.

The double burden is usually view as a primary problem for single women or married women. People fail to recognize that men can and often do go through the same trials and hard times as a parent trying to balance work and the family.

Within the book The Canadian Family in Crisis, Conway addresses this issue with an argument from Eichler. Eichler says, "Social science fails to understand men" by tending "to downplay or ignore a potential conflict between work and home for men." Married men can avoid the full impact of the double burden but single fathers are totally incapable of avoiding the double burden of family and work.

Though single fathers face the same amount of problems that single mothers face, they have two advantages that play in their favor. Men usually have a higher income and have a shorter time of being single than women.

The thing is, until they are remarried or have a woman to help them out around the house, men still must deal with the frustration as a woman does. They must deal with the balancing of work, childcare, and domestic responsibilities. Single fathers are usually doubtful about their ability be a parent, and they are challenged psychologically.

A man being a single parent and feelings the effects of the double burden can and will interfere with his career just as it does with a single mother that has a career. A study showed that five percent of single fathers were fired form their jobs due to the double burden and another eight percent quit because the double burden became too much of a burden for them to balance both work and the family.

With that being said, single fathers feel the same if not more of the effect of the double burden as women do.

The double burden that single mothers endure really comes without much explanation as history has shown, women are likely to end up with this burden. Single mothers usually have higher rates of employment and children at home and have the highest levels overall of the double burden.

Women also have less economic resources than men and have no partner to share the workload with. Single mothers fall heavily under economic vulnerability and one reason is that women's wages are less than seventy percent of men's wages. Single mothers may face job discrimination and not earn as much so it will be even harder on her to maintain the double burden. Single-mother families tend to be creeping around the poverty line with a poverty rate that is twice as high of that for men.

Married Parents

Women take on the largest portion of the domestic obligations of the home, even when they are working full-time jobs. This breeds anger and frustration, as women know they do the majority of the housework on top of their careers.

There have been said to be more reasons, other than gender roles, as to why there is a difference in the housework performed by men and women. Some theories have suggested that women's expectations for household cleanliness are higher than men's.

Women feel like they must be responsible for the condition of the home in a way that men do not. Men do invest most of their time in their careers, but women spend double that time caring for the children, state of the home and taking care of the domestic responsibilities.

In a graph from the U.S. Bureau of Labor Statistics in 2004, that compare the workload of married men and women between the ages of 25-54, women are displayed as performing one hundred percent more housework than men, and men are displayed as having more leisure time than women.

As the double burden increased in 1980, women became more critical of their marriages than men and wanted the men to do more around the house to ease the burden of a second shift. The double burden of women who have jobs and still shoulder

"I'm going to bed."

WIFE	HUSBAND
- Pick up burp cloths & baby clothes all over the house. - Take clothes to laundry room. - Start a load of laundry. - Fold baby clothes from dryer. - Put baby clothes away without waking the baby. - Take out diaper trash bag from diaper pail. - Clean the kitchen. - Pick up the living room. - Check on the baby. - Pump milk. - Label & store milk. - Wash & sterilize breast pump. - Check on the baby. - Walk the dog. - Make sure dog has food & water. - Lock all doors and windows. - Check the AC temperature. - Check on the baby. - Take a shower. - Brush teeth, floss, mouthwash. - Check on the baby. - Get in bed; hear the baby cry. - Go feed baby. - Get back in bed; baby cries again. - Go change baby's diaper. - Go back to bed. - Go to sleep.	- Goes to bed.

the majority of the housework at home leads to women filing or initiating divorce.

Double Burden - A Worldwide Phenomenon

This concept of the double burden with married couples is a worldwide phenomenon. Throughout different cultures of the world,

> On average, women put in 31.5 hours a week of unpaid work across the nations belonging to the OECD (Organisation for Economic Cooperation and Development). Men do just 21 hours of unpaid work, but put in more hours in their day jobs – 33.7 against women's 24.5.
>
> Italy – which has one of the lowest birth rates in the western world – has the biggest gender gap when it comes to carving up chores. Italian women clock up 21 hours more per week than men on housework.
>
> They are followed by Japan (21 hours), India (18 hours), Spain (15 hours), New Zealand, Turkey and Canada (all 14 hours), Korea (13.5 hours) Mexico (13 hours) and France (12.5 hours).
>
> Those with children were described as the most 'time poor'.
>
> Every child generated a reduction in discretionary time for women of 2.3 hours a week but just 1.7 hours for men across the OECD.
>
> Researchers also found women were more likely to multitask by carrying out two domestic tasks at the same time, such as cooking and childcare.
>
> Men, on the other hand, would combine one chore with a 'leisure' task, such as 'looking after the children while reading the newspaper'.
>
> 'As a result, men tend to associate more positive feelings with multitasking than women do,' the report concluded.
>
> But overall women in the OECD countries are spending less time on housework than they were a decade ago, dropping 2.6 hours a week while bumping up their time at the office by one hour.
>
> Men's paid work, meanwhile, has decreased by 4.5 hours a week and they have increased the time spent on domestic chores by two hours.
>
> Women are also now more likely to hire cleaners, nannies or childminders while buying more ready meals or eating out to cut down on the amount of time spent on unpaid household tasks.
>
> ~ Report by Organisation for Economic Cooperation And Development (OECD, November 2013)

women spend more total hours in work than men do. In Japan, once married, they are still expected to be devoted wives and mothers who give all off their effort to the home, even after a full day of work.

Latin American women, now entering the work force in large numbers, still face what they call doble jornada, or double day's journey. Although in the Latin American culture, men are starting to interact more with the children and helping around the house more, the main domestic responsibilities still fall upon the women of the house.

Sometimes women who are primary wage earners are still relegated to most of the domestic work. European men are more likely to play and interact with their children but not likely to participate fully in their daily care. They are more likely to help their wives at home, yet rarely do they tackle all domestic task equally.

Men commonly fail to live up to their belief of equal sharing of domestic labor: they may believe in an equal workload in the house, but the inconvenience of taking on work done by their wives stops many from following through.

Effects of double burden

Stress

When faced with the double burden of having to deal with the responsibilities of both a career as well as domestic duties, sometimes a person's health is affected. Many people faced with these circumstances have a higher chance of being sick since health and stress seem to be correlated, as stress has been implicated in up to eighty percent of all illnesses, as found by a report done by the Canadian Advisory Council on the Status of Women.

In an article that was written by a team of researchers it was found that both men and women faced with a "spillover" of work and family issues were 1.5-1.6 times more likely to have an absence due to sickness than others. Men and women in these situations have also been proven to be more likely to be faced with psychological stress and even see themselves as unhealthier than their colleagues who are not in their situation.

Mortality Rate

In a study done by Rosamund Weatherall, Heather Joshi and Susan Macran of the London School of Hygiene and Tropical Medicine in 1994, the research presented suggests that women who had part-time jobs had a mortality rate lower than the women with full-time jobs and children.

Absences Due To Sickness

In several Western countries it has been seen that absences due to sickness for women are far greater than men. When investigating the reasons behind this, a study done in Sweden published in 1996 found that half of the difference between genders can be dismissed if you take out the days missed by pregnant women.

When taking into account the health effects of double burden, child birth is always a possibility for mothers who already are faced with taking care of children and having a career that affects them and their health.

'Decades of tradition have been overturned. I've taken over your armchair'

In many studies people have tried to relate the difference in sickness absences directly to the double burden effect. It has been somewhat successful as women who are faced with work and child care have been known to request more sick days than men in the same situation. Additionally, working wives with children have twice the absence rate as men who are placed in the same position in work family conflicts.

Loss Of Sleep

The stress of maintaining a career and a household can also lead to a loss of sleep. In traditional gender roles it is usually the mother who is the one to get the family going in the morning as she fixes breakfast and takes the children to school before she goes to her own job.

At night the mother cooks and does various other activities around the house that cause her to be the last person to retire for the night as well. Although this is merely just a few gender roles that are not set in stone, they may hold to be true.

It was found that working women sleep twenty-five minutes less a night due solely to their responsibility for domestic work. Applying this statistic in larger scale leads to the assumption that women on average lose up to thirteen hours of sleep per month due to domestic duties. It can be assumed that it is possible for an average woman to lose up to one hundred and fifty-six hours of sleep during a year because of domestic work and motherly duties.

Work Intensity

For many poor women and men whose work hours have reached the point where they cannot cut back on leisure time anymore to make time for domestic and paid work, work intensity is an issue because they often intensify their work time by doing two or more activities at once, such as taking care of children while cooking. Work intensity can lead to many negative health consequences, such as lack of sleep, stress, and lack of recreation.

> *A woman's real business is to look after household affairs, keep everything neat and clean, and if there is sufficient milk supply available, she should always be engaged in churning butter, making yogurt, curd, so many nice varieties, simply from milk. The woman should be cleaning, sewing, like that.*
> *-Srila Prabhupada (Letter to female disciple, February 16, 1972)*

Economic Effects

There are many economic effects on the person who has to shoulder the double burden. According to Himmelweit (2002), because women often earn less than men, there is the thought that the woman should be the one to fit her paid job around household activities such as taking care of children. Because of this, and because they have many domestic duties, women often take part-time jobs and jobs in the informal sector in order to balance paid work with domestic work.

Part-time jobs and jobs in the informal sector do earn less than full-time jobs, so men have to increase their paid work hours in order to compensate for the lacking family income. This will "weaken her earning power and strengthen his", leading to an unequal distribution of power in the household, and allow the man to exploit the woman's unpaid work.

This situation could have negative consequences especially for the woman because she is perceived to have less contribution to the household, due to domestic work being seen as less of a contribution than paid work.

Though wanting at times, such woman does not have the economic means to ask for a divorce because she does not have a full-time job, and she has less money that she personally receives, decreasing her perceived contributions to the household.

Source
Gerri Peev, The Daily Mail, 5 November 2013
Wikipedia
Phyllis Moen (1989). Working Parents. University of Wisconsin Press. p. 4.
Hochschild, Arlie and Anne Machung. 1990. The Second Shift. Avon Books: New York.
Vaananen, Ari; May V. Kevin; Leena Ala-Mursula; Jaana Pentti; Mika Kivimaki; Jussi Vahtera (2004). "The Double Burden of and Negative Spillover Between Paid

and Domestic Work: Associations with Health Among Men and Women". Women & Health 40 (3)

Hakim, Catherine. "(How) can social policy and fiscal policy recognise unpaid family work?".

Himmelweit, Susan (2002). "Making visible the hidden economy: the case for gender-impact analysis of economic policy". Feminist Economics (Taylor and Francis) 8 (1)

Suzana Smith and Diana Converse. Double Day Work: How Women Cope With Time Demands. University of Florida, IFAS Extension.

Acemoglu, Daron, David H. Autor, David Lyle. "Women, War, and Wages: The Effect of Female Labor Supply on the Wage Structure at Midcentury"

Rosenfeld, Rachel A. 1996. "Women's Work Histories". Population and Development Review.

Siegelbaum, Lewis. "1968: The Double Burden".

Conway, John Fredrick (2003). The Canadian Family in Crisis. James Lorimer & Company. pp. 213–232.

Lourdes Beneria (2008). The Crisis of Care, International Migration, and Public Policy. Feminist Economics.

Martha Alter Chen. Women in the informal sector: A global picture, the global movement, Radcliffe Institute for Advanced Study. Retrieved from: http://www.cpahq.org/cpahq/cpadocs/module6mc.pdf

Hilary Abell (1999). Endangering Women's Health for Profit: Health and Safety in Mexico's Maquiladoras. Development in Practice, 9(5), 595-600.

Sarah Gammage (2010). Time Pressed and Time Poor: Unpaid Household Work in Guatemala, Feminist Economics.

Latapi, A. E., & Rocha, M. G. (2008). Girls, Mothers, and Poverty Reduction in Mexico: Evaluating Progresa-Oportunidades. In S. Razavi (ed.), The Gendered Impacts of Liberalization: Towards Embedded Liberalism? pp:435-468. New York, 2008.

Martha Chen, Joann Vanek, Francie Lund, James Heintz with Renana Jhabvala, Christine Bonner (2005). Progress of the World's Women. UN Women.

Elena Bardasi & Quentil Wodon, (2010). Working Long Hours and Having No Choice: Time Poverty in Guinea, Feminist Economics, 16(3), 45-78.

Roberta Guerrina (2002). Mothering in Europe: Feminist Critique of European Policies on Motherhood and Employment, European Journal of Women Studies 9(1).

(2013). The Global Gender Gap Report, World Economic Forum.

Molyneux, M. (1995). Superwomen and the Double Burden: Women's Experience of Change in Central and Eastern Europe and the Former Soviet Union. Feminist Studies, (3), 637.

Roudakova, N., Ballard-Reisch, D. (1999). Femininity and the Double Burden: Dialogues on the Socialization of Russian Daughters into Womanhood. Anthropology of East Europe Review

Jeemol Unni, (2004). Globalization and Securing Rights for Women Informal Workers in Asia, Journal of Human Development, 5(3).

(2012). Women Matter: An Asian Perspective, McKinsey & Company.

Maria S. Floro & Anant Pichetpongsa (2010). Gender, Work Intensity, and Well-Being of Thai Home-Based Workers, Feminist Economics.

Chesters, Jenny. 2012. "Gender Attitudes and Housework: Trends over Time in Australia". Journal of Comparative Family Studies.

World Survey. 2009. "Access to Full Employment and Decent Work". p 27-40.

Lulie Aslaksen, Charlotte Koren & Marianne Stokstad (2000). The Effect of Child Care Subsidies: A Critique of the Rosen Model, Feminist Economics, 6(1).

Carmen Sirianni & Cynthia Negrey (2000). Working Time as Gendered Time, Feminist Economics, 6(1).

Jen Roesch, (2004). Turning back the clock? Women, work, and family today, International Socialist Review.

Natalie Chen, Paola Conconi and Carlo Perroni, (2007). Women's Earning Power and the "Double Burden" of Market and Household Work, University of Warwick.

Barbara Petrongolo, (2004). Gender segregation in employment contracts. Journal Of The European Economic Association, 2(2/3), 331-345.

Tamara Hervey and Jo Shaw, (1998). Women, Work and Care: Women's Dual Role and Double Burden in Ec Sex Equality Law, Journal of European Social Policy 8(43).

Maria Sagrario Floro (1995). Women's well-being, poverty, and work intensity, Feminist Economics, 1(3).

UNICEF. 2007. The State of the World's Children. New York: United Nations Children's Fund.

De Ferranti, David. 2004. Inequality in Latin American and the Caribbean: Breaking with History?. World Bank, Mexico.

Hobson, Barbara Meil (2002). Making Men Into Fathers: men, masculinities, and the social politics of fatherhood. Cambridge University Press. p. 36.

Bratberg, Espen; Svenn-Age Dahl and Alf Erling Risa (2002). European Sociological Review 18 (2): 233–249.

Landsman, Paige (1994). "Juggling Work And Family Flexible Scheduling, And Changing Attitudes Help Balance Demands.". Business Insurance: 16.

The Cambridge Reporter (2001). "Juggling work and family.". The Montreal Gazette: A4.

Mwangi, Sophia (2008). "Juggling that perfect 'art'; If you're a wife and a mother, if you're a mother on her own or if you're the husband, then you will identify with the 'art' that I am going to talk about. I hope we can all celebrate the joys this 'art' bestows.". New African: 78.

Glicksman, Eve (Sep 12, 1996), "Juggling School and Family", Jewish Exponent 200 (11): 47

Ryan, Kathleen O. (Nov 9, 1994), "90s FAMILY Back to the Books Parents are taking to the classroom again-but this time, they're juggling work, school and family", Los Angeles Times: 3

Weiss, Barbara (2004). "Back to school? Nurses say: you bet! Juggling work, school, and family is a long, hard journey, but many nurses who take this route find it well worth the effort.". RN 67 (7): 63.

Ryff, Carol (1996). The Parental Experience in Midlife. Chicago, Illinois: The University of Chicago Press. p. 658.

Sernau, Scott (2006). Worlds Apart: Social Inequalities. California: Pine Forge Press. pp. 158–161.

Young, Brigitte (1999). Triumph of the Fatherland. Michigan: University of Michigan Press. p. 277.

Weatherall, Rosamund; Heather Joshi and Susan Macran (1994). "Double Burden or Double Blessing? Employment, Motherhood and Mortality in the Longitudinal Study of England and Wales".

Ann Ferguson (2010). Feminist Perspectives on Class and Work, Stanford Encyclopedia of Philosophy.

6

Working Mothers

Trapped By 'Double Burden' Of Guilt

Working mothers are paralysed by a 'double burden' of guilt, which make them anxious about neglecting their children and concerned that motherhood makes them worse employees. They feel they are being bad mothers for going to work and bad workers when they put their children first, a study has shown.

Researchers found women spend far more time agonising about their jobs at home and more time worrying about their families at work, than men do.

Shira Offer, an assistant professor in the Department of Sociology and Anthropology at Bar-Ilan University in Israel, studied the work life balance of hundreds of families.

IT IS HARD TO BE A WOMAN
*You must think like a man,
Act like a lady.
Look like a young girl,
And work like a horse.*

She asked 402 American mothers and 291 fathers in families where they both worked to complete a survey and a time and emotions diary.

The study found that working mothers engaged in 'mental labour' in about one fourth, and working fathers in one fifth, of their waking time.

'Mental labour' is defined as worrying about something - be it work, or family life - which can impair performance and make it difficult to focus.

Mothers were found to worry for five hours a week more than men and spend more time being anxious about work when they were with the family. Men seemed to be able to switch-off from the office more easily.

Asst Prof Offer said: "We know that mothers are the ones who usually adjust their work schedule to meet family demands, such as staying home with a sick child.

"Therefore, mothers may feel that they do not devote enough time to their job and have to 'catch up,' and, as a result, they are easily preoccupied with job-related matters outside the workplace.

"This illustrates the double burden, the pressure to be 'good' mothers and 'good' workers, that working mums experience."

Working mothers worry far more about their jobs when they are home with their families than men do

Women were found to engage in worrying about work or family problems for 29 hours a week compared to men at 24 hours.

When they were at home men worried about work matters around 25 per cent of the time, compared with women who worried about their jobs for 34 per cent of the time.

Asst Prof Offer added: "I thought that highly educated fathers holding professional and managerial positions would often be

Career Woman - The Violence of Modern Jobs And The Lost Art of Home Making

preoccupied with job matters when doing things such as housework or during their free time.

"It appears, however, that fathers are quite adept at leaving their work concerns behind and are better able to draw boundaries between work and home.

"I believe that fathers can afford to do that because someone else, namely their spouse, assumes the major responsibility for the household and childcare."

She added: "It is true that fathers today are more involved in childrearing and do more housework than in previous generations, but the major responsibility for the domestic realm continues to disproportionately fall on mothers' shoulders and this has to change."

The study was presented to the American Sociological Association.

Source
Sarah Knapton, Science Correspondent, The Telegraph, 19 Feb 2014

Women claim to be equal, so that now they are thinking that they do not want to become pregnant, so they are killing their own child. What kind of equality is this that it creates another's suffering? As soon as the body is different how can there be equality? We see that a woman cannot work so hard as a man, and women can do work that a man cannot do, so where is there equality?"
~ Srila Prabhupada (Letter to Ed Gilbert, 9th September, 1975)

7

Stress Of A Career

Leading To Smoking And Drinking, Harming Women's Health

Life Expectancy Gap Between The Sexes Is Narrowing Rapidly

Women are losing their lead over men in life expectancy as they trade homemaking for careers.

Work stress – and related drinking and smoking – are taking an increasing toll on their health, according to the Office for National Statistics (ONS), London.

In 1963 men were twice as likely to die early as women. Last year however the increased risk fell to one and a half times and the life expectancy gap has fallen from six years to fewer than four.

The ONS study is the first official recognition that women who have abandoned the domestic lives of their grandmothers now face the same shorter lifespans of men.

'Ministers want women to work long hours

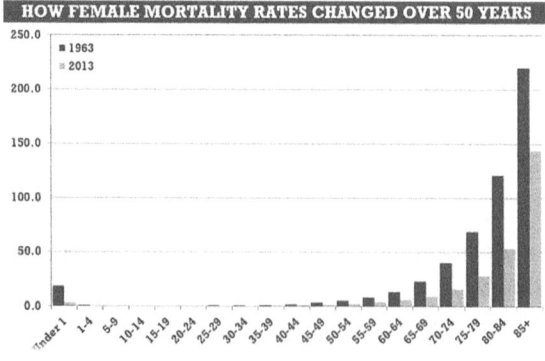

HOW FEMALE MORTALITY RATES CHANGED OVER 50 YEARS

52

when they have children, but these figures…indicates there may be public health problems as a result,' says Laura Perrins of the pressure group 'Mothers at Home Matter'.

'There is clearly now a health interest in providing transferable tax allowances that would make it possible for people to stay at home with young children.'

Higher premature death rates for women were most marked in the 55 to 69 age group, the paper found.

'Increases in women entering the labour force over the last 50 years are considered to have had an impact on stress, smoking and drinking, leading to changes in the health of females,' says the ONS.

According to ONS, male health had improved with lower smoking and drinking rates and fewer dangerous jobs in industrial environments.

Two years ago ONS research found for the first time since the Victorian age that mortality rates were not improving among some groups of working women. They cited the 'intermediate' group that includes saleswomen, counter clerks, clerical workers in the public sector and medical and dental technicians.

The move towards millions of women going out to work 'has had a negative impact on their health'

Women have always enjoyed greater life expectancy.

But in recent years, the gap between the sexes has been closing. Life expectancy for a child born between 2011 and 2013 went up to 78.9 for a boy and 82.7 for a girl, leaving a gap between the sexes of 3.8 years. However in the early 1980s life expectancy gap was six years.

Women have been increasingly adopting risky habits to the same level as men.

In the mid-1970s, half of all men smoked but only four in ten women. By 2011 overall numbers of smokers had dropped, but women smoked nearly as much as men – 19 per cent against 21 per cent.

State surveys also show that while levels of drinking are falling overall, they are falling at a slower rate for women than men. In 2011, 57 per cent of men were drinking at least once a week, against 54 per cent of women, with the gap halved over a period of just six years.

Smoking and drinking levels have risen with the advance of women into working lives, a revolution in the lives of millions which has also resulted in women marrying later in life, if at all. The average age at which a woman has a child is now over 30, and numbers of women having children in their 40s has risen fivefold since the 1970s.

Some analysts link higher stress levels in working women with the sharp rise in numbers who go to work while they have young families. Official figures this year showed the number of stay-at-

Career Woman - The Violence of Modern Jobs And The Lost Art of Home Making

The move towards millions of women going out to work 'has had a negative impact on their health'

home mothers has dropped to just over two million, down from three million 20 years ago.

Researcher and author Patricia Morgan said: 'Men's life expectancy has been increasing in the way that could be predicted, because of less going down coal mines or falling off scaffolding.

'However government policies that have put pressure on women to work, whether they want to or not, may not have been entirely a good thing. We may be looking at the unintended consequences of the economic pressure on women to go out to work throughout their lives.'

Source
Steve Doughty, Social Affairs Correspondent, The Daily Mail
13 October 2014

Daily Juggling Acts Crippling Modern Women

Modern women are struggling to cope with more than six different roles to get through their lives everyday, according to a new study.

The study by tea maker Twinings found that as well as being a friend, cook, housekeeper and mother, they are also a daughter, employee and colleague, lover, agony aunt, driver and personal assistant, the Daily Express reported.

Their average 6.2 jobs compare with 4.7 for men who become friend, driver, repair/handyman and father.

As a result, 97 per cent admit they feel stressed with one in 10 feeling 'so stressed out they can't remember what it feels like to be calm or content'.

Working Mom Quiz:
What's Wrong Here?

a. She's going to spill coffee on her laptop
b. Her car keys are in her hand, not the bottom of her bag
c. Earrings? Who has time to put on earrings?
d. All of the above

A third of women turn to wine or overeat as a means to unwind.

Source
ANI, Oct 22, 2011

Poor woman, helpless, no father, no husband, no son. This is the civilization. They are forlorn, and they are forced to take the profession of... What is that? What is that advertisement? Forget... Up and down...?

Hari-sauri: Topless, bottomless. They are forced to dancing halls.

Prabhupada: Just see. ...no means, either welfare or topless dance. No father, no son, no husband. That's civilization? Rascal civilization. They should be given protection. This is Vedic civilization. Na striya svatantryam arha... They must be given... Like children, they must be given protection. No father. Father-mother divorce. She is alone. Then no husband, no children. What is this civilization? Always helpless. I have seen so many old women feeling helpless. Yes. Oh, yes.

Hari-sauri: They stick them in a home now.

Prabhupada: And on account of their helplessness, these rascals are enjoying: "Come here in the club, in the shop." Advertise, "Topless, bottomless." This is going on. And they claim to be civilized.

Hari-sauri: You said in that article in the BTG that women's liberation means that they get more exploited.

Prabhupada: Yes. The giving them bluff that "You become liberated" means "We shall exploit you, young girls." This is the idea behind. Because the karmis, they want sex, young girls, and they get energy to work. The Europeans, Americans, they work so hard. They get energy from new, new girls. This is psychology, Therefore they work like hogs and dogs. Dog civilization. Hog civilization. Because the hog has no restriction, either mother, sister, or anyone, "Come on." And here is the civilization. Tapo divyam. Be brahmacari, undergo austerities and rectify your, this conditioned life, birth and death. This is human civilization. Why you are under birth and death? One life remain brahmacari and solve all the question. Tyaktva deham punar janma naiti [Bg. 4.9]. Teach them, these rascals that this is civilization. It is not civilization to work hard like hogs and dogs and have sex enjoyment.

~ Srila Prabhupada (Walk -- January 24, 1977, Bhuvanesvara)

9

Modern India

Killing Its Urban Working Women

Conflicting values of an ancient and modern India have come together to create a dangerous environment for working urban women. While they're still expected to dispense their traditional duties of being a wife, mother, daughter-in-law or mother-in-law, now working women are also expected to bring in the bread. They're expected to keep the house clean, cook and dispense other wifely duties while navigating the complex corporate structure. And all this is taking a toll on their health. And given most middle-aged men have grown up in an era where they grew up seeing their mothers do all the household work, the concept of giving a helping hand isn't really there in most middle-class Indian families.

Three out of four working women in India suffer from lifestyle, chronic or acute ailments due to the pressure from trying to balance their personal and professional lives, according to an Assocham survey. The survey findings, released ahead of International Women's Day on March 8, reveals that 42 per cent of working women suffer from lifestyle diseases like backache, obesity, depression, diabetes, hyper-tension and heart ailments.

Besides, twenty-two per cent of women surveyed suffered from chronic diseases while 14 per cent had acute ailments. 'Working women have to double up as valued employees at their work place and home-makers after office hours. This takes a toll on their health,' says D S Rawat, Assocham Secretary General.

The survey was conducted on 2,800 working women aged between 32-58 years from 120 companies across 11 sectors of the economy in 10 cities - Ahmedabad, Bangalore, Chennai, Delhi-NCR, Hyderabad, Jaipur, Kolkata, Lucknow, Mumbai and Pune.

Marriage - Changing Priorities

Marriage marks a palpable shift not only in the life of women, but also in the way they view their priorities. One of the examples is her career that moves down from first to fourth place after becoming a daughter-in-law, says a survey conducted by one of the leading matrimonial sites. On the occasion of International Women's Day on March 8, Jeevansathi.com has done a survey to understand woman's priorities in life before and after marriage.

The survey was conducted on more than 1,500 women, who were asked to rank their priorities in life before matrimony and post wedding. Career and job were given number one spot with 53 percent of women putting it as their number one concern. The tables turned post the walk down the aisle with women ranking career as number four priority. So when asked about priorities after marriage, 51 percent of women indicated their future partner as their number one priority.

'The survey clearly shows a tangible shift in women's priorities before and after marriage and also throws light on the outlook of women towards their lives. Indian women have pristine clarity towards what they value most in life with career and husband becoming their top priorities before and after marriage,' says Prakash Sangam, business head, Jeevansathi.com. Also, 25 percent of women ranked their parents as the number two priority in their lives before marriage. But an equal number of women ranked their parents as number three priority after marriage since their own children take up the second place in the priority list. Money featured on number three in their priority list before marriage, while post marriage it is filial duties that take precedence over monetary concerns. The survey also says that post marriage, Indian women hardly spend time on their hobbies and travelling.

Source
Nirmalya Dutta Mar 07, 2014, March 8 is International Women's Day.
With inputs from IANS and PTI

Several press reports with similar theme are produced below to highlight the gravity of the issue.

3/4th Of Working Women Suffering From Life Style Ailment: Survey

Rohith BR, TNN | Mar 7, 2014, Times of India

Daily 'multitask' requirement on working women is taking a toll on their health severely. This has been revealed in a recent survey done by the Associated Chamber of Commerce and Industry (ASSOCHAM). The study says three-fourth of them in the age group of 32-58 suffering from some life-style, chronic and acute ailment.

The survey said women were found to be afflicted with lifestyle, chronic and acute ailments such as obesity, depression, chronic backache, diabetes, hypertension, high cholesterol, heart, kidney disease etc. Those in the younger age bracket manage to cope up but are in a danger of slipping into the health problems, it said.

The survey also found that about 42 per cent of working women were found to be suffering from lifestyle diseases like backache, obesity, depression, diabetes, hyper-tension and heart ailments.

"Twenty-two per cent of women taken in the sample survey were reported to be suffering from chronic diseases and 14 per cent of the women had acute ailments," it added.

Working Women - Fighting A Losing Battle

By K. S. Harikrishnan, Thiruvananthapuram, India, Nov 19 2012, Inter Press Service (IPS)

Sreelakshmi, an office executive in a major diagnostic laboratory in Thiruvananthapuram, the capital city of the southern Indian state of Kerala, ends her 11-hour working day to return home at night to a mountain of domestic chores.

At 35, she is already diabetic and vulnerable to disorders ranging from obesity and depression to hypertension and chronic backache.

Health experts warn that Sreelakshmi represents an increasing number of high-powered Indian working women who juggle workplace and domestic responsibilities in an effort to keep everyone around them happy, while disregarding the toll this hectic lifestyle takes on their minds and bodies.

For ambitious, middle-class women such as Sreelakshmi, hailing from a suburban area of Thiruvananthapuram, the office and the home are equally important: they cannot afford to choose one over the other. The result is a harmful mix of stress, anxiety and exhaustion.

"Women in the age group of 20-40 are more prone to lifestyle diseases. Today women tend to give more importance to their careers rather than their own health. Work pressures lead them to eat more of junk food which leads to obesity and other health related issues. Lack of time forces them to get less amount and poor quality of sleep. A busy lifestyle results in lack of exercise and poor nutrition resulting in iron and calcium deficiency. Irritation and mental depression become a part of their lives which in turn badly affects the hormones that play a vital role in a woman's body. Hormonal disturbances increase with stress and then result in ovulation and polycystic ovarian diseases", says a Gynaecologist from Mumbai.

~ Ekta Bhatnagar, Assocham.org

Career Woman - The Violence of Modern Jobs And The Lost Art of Home Making

Dr. Manjula, a senior medical scientist at the government health institute in Thiruvananthapuram, told IPS that many working women are suffering from "lifestyle diseases".

A survey conducted by the Mumbai-based Associated Chamber of Commerce and Industry (ASSOCHAM) in 2009 revealed that 68 percent of working women suffer from lifestyle diseases like obesity, diabetes and depression.

Elaborating on the health challenges facing Indian working women, Dr. Mohan Rao, a professor at the Centre for Social Medicine and Community Health at the Delhi-based Jawaharlal Nehru University, told IPS that hunger, anaemia and infectious diseases remain the major epidemiological priorities for working women in India, the majority of whom are in the unorganised sector, working for low wages.

"That's nothing, you want to try juggling three kids and a full time job."

"The working woman struggles between the responsibilities of production and reproduction. They often sacrifice their own health

> *Male chauvinist. Patriarchal Hindu survey. Women should not be afraid of all these illnesses. They should focus on becoming independent of men by becoming financially independent. Women can always buy medicines made by women and empower medical women. If men are suffering the same problems, let them buy medicines made by women too. Long live the corporates who empower women. If you have a daughter make sure the corporates make her work 12 hrs a day...just like the men. Then she will prove to the world that women are empowered.*
>
> *~ Shanti Iyer (Delhi)*

for the health of the family," he said. "We need to improve the public health system so that women have access to (a range of) healthcare facilities, and not merely reproductive health services. But we also need to improve working conditions, wages (and) provide access to the universal public distribution systems," he added.

A survey entitled 'Rising Workplace Obesity Among Indian Women', conducted by Healthji.com in association with Leisa's Secret, a firm that sells weight-loss products, revealed that about 80 percent of urban working women in the 25-45 age group are experiencing weight gains as a result of a sedentary lifestyle.

"Most women (say) they lack the time to walk or exercise due to work pressure," according to Heal Foundation President R. Shankar.

Dr. Sreelekha Nair, researcher at the Centre for Women's Development Studies in New Delhi, told IPS that the health problems arising from a sedentary life style have reached pandemic levels, with far-reaching economic, environmental and social consequences.

Depression is another major challenge for working women.

Working Women - Toll of Multiple Roles
Lifestyle diseases also depend on the kind of sector one is working in. Women in the Media sector, BPO's, touring jobs are more prone to lifestyle diseases as these sectors are much more demanding of one's time. One of the main reasons for a stressful life is the falling nutritional level which eats away into the immune system.

"Being a journalist my working hours are not defined. I have to travel a lot and do a lot of running around and late nights to file a story and eat whatever I can lay my hands on. On top of that one has to attend all social events to stay in the crowd. This does leave me feeling tired and stressed at the end of the day. I feel lethargic and fall sick easily but still have to go to work as we can't afford to take leave every time. I work six days a week and even on that one day off that I get, I have to finish all the household chores. I don't get time to spend on my health or to look after myself", comments a media professional.

~ Ekta Bhatnagar, Assocham.org

Psychiatrists say the inability to perform as well as expected in the workplace, non-achievement of targets, missing deadlines and constant worry about shirking family responsibilities could lead to clinical depression.

Dr. Roy Kuruvila, a well-known psychiatrist in Chennai, told IPS that stressful working environments affect women more than men, as the former have fewer outlets for venting their anxiety or frustration.

"Social support and encouragement are needed to decrease the tensions of working women," he added.

> *What do you mean by "successfully living"? Successfully living does not mean that you work hard just like cats and dogs, and eat something and have sex life at night. That is not successful life. That successful life is there even in the cats and dogs and hogs. The hogs are also laboring very hard. The cats and dogs, they are also roaming around for their food. And the sex is there. Everything is there. That is not successful life. Real successful life is how to understand one's real constitutional position as part and parcel of the Supreme Lord. That is successful life. This is not successful life. What is this successful life? I see... I have got so many students. They are well-qualified. But they have got... When they work, they have to work so hard, they go at six o'clock to the working and comes again at six o'clock, all day, tired. They lost all vitality, all sense. Is that successful life, simply for one morsel of food, working so hard? And unless one works so hard, he cannot eat. We have created a civilization that one must earn thousands of dollars, then he can live like a gentleman. Is that successful life? And for earning that thousands of dollars he has to work so hard, just like an animal, beast. No. That is not successful life. Successful life is that, that we should make our bodily necessities of life as far as required, not more than that. I want to eat something. God has given sufficient food. You grow. You live anywhere. You grow foodstuff. You grow grains. You grow fruits. You grow vegetables. Keep cows. Take milk. You can live anywhere. You haven't got to go fifty miles off with a car to attend your office at six o'clock with velocity of hundred miles' speed. Is that successful life, do you think? So where is the successful life? We are proposing successful life.*
>
> *~ Srila Prabhupada (Lecture -- Hawaii, March 23, 1969)*

The problem reaches deep into family life, impacting parenting as well. A five-member study team, led by Dr. M.K.C. Nair, director of the Child Development Centre in the Government Medical College in Thiruvananthapuram, found that there was less breastfeeding among working mothers than non-working mothers.

"An exclusive breastfeeding rate of 54.28 percent was reported among non-working mothers and a much lower rate, 29.52 percent, among working mothers." Over 77 percent of "working women quoted lack of maternity leave beyond three months as the major impediment to exclusive breast feeding", the study found.

Doctors practicing the Indian Systems of Medicine opine that most working women avoid routine check-ups due to time constraints. They advise women to keep a careful watch for endometriosis, breast cancer, cervical spondylosis, insomnia, hypothyroidism and hair loss.

Dr. V.S. Ambal, a physician at the Santhigiri Health Care Research Centre at Pothencode in Thiruvananthapuram, said that excess work also leads to menstrual disorders and other gynaecological problems.

"Ayurveda disallows disparate food combinations, which damage internal organs, and advises the intake of natural food. There has been a major shift in the food habits of working women in cities, who prefer to have fast and packaged food due to work pressure, standard of living and convenience," she told IPS.

Studies and surveys suggest that consumption of fast foods, which contain a high percentage of salt, sugar and preservatives, is on the rise.

An ASSOCHAM survey conducted this year revealed that 67 percent of working women admitted to switching away from traditional food items that are nutritious, simple and easy to digest to fast foods loaded with empty calories. Even 'An apple a day, keeps the doctor away', this may not necessarily hold true in today's busy scenario, especially for women.

10

Diabetes

More Common in Stressed Out, Working Women

Working women who are stressed out at work are "more likely to turn to foods with higher fat and sugar content than men." This is Peter Smith's conclusion from a study he led evaluating the behaviour of men and women in the workplace.

The study "was based on data on 7,443 people taken from the 2000-01 Canadian Community Health Survey and linked to statistics of the number of doctor visits and hospital admissions. Those individuals never had diabetes, were not self-employed and had worked more than 10 hours a week for more than 20 weeks over a year."

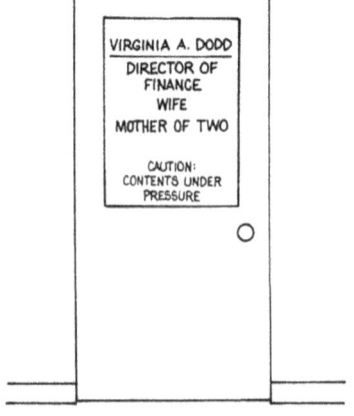

The results showed that 19 percent of cases of diabetes in women were due to low job control. This number is higher than that of smoking, drinking or low physical activity but lower than that of obesity.

Smith believes that the differences lie in the way men and women deal with stress in the workplace. While women are more likely to turn to unhealthy food for relief, men are more likely to turn to other forms of relief like working out and running.

"Men and women react differently to workplace stress," he says while one of the study's coauthors, Dr. Richard Glazier explains that stressful situations "take a toll on the body and they really affect how the body handles sugars and fats and can lead toward the development of obesity and Type 2 diabetes."

Source
Angela Ayles, August 22, 2012, CBC.ca

Kastan kaman means with hard labor to satisfy the four necessities of life. The four necessities of life I have already mentioned: eating, sleeping, sex life, and defense. These are bodily necessities. So the hog or the pig is also trying to maintain his body. You have no experience. In India we have got experience. In the villages there are hogs. Day and night, they are loitering in the street, and when they find out some stool, they are very happy. Therefore this animal has been especially mentioned, that "Do you spoil your life like the hog, working day and night, night duty, work day duty and this duty, that duty, and what is the gain? You get some food which may not be very nice and eat it. And then you satisfy your sex." Is that life very perfect life? That is being done by the hogs also.

~ Srila Prabhupada (Srimad-Bhagavatam 6.1.3 -- Melbourne, May 22, 1975)

11
Working Women

And Their Back Pain Woes

Ouch! It is that hurting back again. You pause a second, dismiss the dull ache with a mental shake of the head and get back to the project with a looming deadline. Alas, majority of the working women struggle with back pain. Weighed down by heavy workloads and long working hours in the office coupled with the strenuous demands of household chores takes its toll on the body and the first casualty is more often than not, the spinal column.

Most women experience some sort of back pain at some point during their working lives. So much so that, back pain is the most common cause of job-related disability and a leading contributor to missed work (especially female employees under 40-years). It is one of the most common neurological ailments and ranks as the number two reason why women see their family doctor!

Prof. Lavu Narendranath of Nizam's Institute of Medical Sciences (Orthopaedic department) says, "At least two to three working women suffering from back pain consult us daily. There is a significant rise in number in last three to four years!"

Yet, it is difficult to pinpoint an exact cause for back pain. The problem can stem from a variety of factors ranging from muscle strain, sprain or spasm due to wrong body posture, poor sleeping position, lifting heavy objects or even daily activities to previous damage or injury to the spine, bones, muscles or nerves. To top it, even excessive emotional stress can cause physical symptoms like back pain to appear which is referred to as psychosomatic back pain.

Despite the varied possible factors, the medical fraternity unanimously blame the working environment of sedentary jobs where women have to sit continuously for hours together. While sitting cannot be considered as 'backbreaking', it does exert maximum pressure on the discs in the spine thus increasing the risk of back problems. The statistics speak for themselves - at least 3 out of every 15 women suffering from back pain are employed in BPOs!

Don't let it go unchecked

The constant discomfort of back pain affects the normal quality of life and throws it out of gear. It becomes difficult to concentrate on work – or anything else for that matter— and recurring pain can lead to increased absenteeism as well. At a point, even routine daily activities turn cumbersome.

The lower back is the most afflicted, with the pain either being a shooting, stabbing, throbbing one or settling in as a persistent dull ache. Be it mild or acute, if neglected, can soon aggravate into a chronic and even crippling one. The strain can leave the sufferer bed-ridden or escalate into serious conditions like slip disc.

Ignore the 'mildly irritant' but lingering back pain at your own peril! It is best to consult an orthopaedic doctor for a proper professional assessment and diagnosis with X-ray, MRI and other tests.

Proper attention and care

Even if the cause is not obvious, most back pain issues respond well to home remedies, over-the-counter medications and even

"I kept ignoring the growing pain in my lower back till one morning I just couldn't get up from the bed. It took a very long time to heal and longer till I could return to my normal duties and life. Now I know better and am extremely careful when it comes to my back!"

~ Anita Jhunjhunwala, proprietor, Kaagaz Krafts

simple lifestyle changes. Maintaining good posture is extremely important – stand up straight, don't slouch when sitting and sleep in the right position on a firm surface. Sit back comfortably (not leaning forward) with your feet resting on the floor (not dangling) or try resting one foot on a low stool to reduce the strain on the spine. Take regular breaks to stand, stretch and move around a bit.

Avoid wearing high heels and sitting in low, deep chairs that are difficult to get out of. Always bend down at the knees and not from the waist. Be extremely careful when picking up a child and avoid carrying a heavy bag on the shoulder (switch sides if needed).

Maintain proper nutrition and diet to reduce and prevent excessive weight. A diet with sufficient daily intake of calcium, phosphorus and vitamin D helps to promote new bone growth. Alternative hot/cold therapy with cold packs and heating pad, massage, soaking in a hot tub or wearing a belt support can numb the soreness for a while. Sometimes taking proper bed rest (2-3 days) and lying straight on your back is all that is needed.

While the above treatments/medications can provide only temporary relief, a regular, age-appropriate exercise program - designed to strengthen lower back and abdominal muscles and tailored to your unique needs and situation can reduce the frequency, intensity and even extinguish back pain completely. You can opt for stretches, low-impact aerobics, strength training, speed walking, swimming or yoga that will strengthen the back muscles and also prevent future problems. But it is advisable to do it under medical supervision or with a qualified personal trainer.

Physiotherapy may become essential to alleviate chronic back pain. Some people also opt for alternative therapies like acupressure, acupuncture or chiropractic care. In extreme cases, surgical treatment is the only option.

Working women may be no stranger to back pain, but it does not necessarily have to go with the territory as 'part of the job'. Take care and keep your back healthy for a comfortable life!

Source
Payal Chanania, The Hindu, February 15, 2012

In the Bhagavad-gita it is plainly said, mudha. He does not know his own interest. He is called mudha, ass. Just like an ass. Ass is whole day working with tons of cloth on his back, but he does not... Not a piece of cloth belongs to him. This is ass. And he is working so hard only for a morsel of grass, which is available everywhere. But he is thinking that "This gentleman, washerman, is giving me food." This is ass. Such food can be available anywhere and everywhere, but he is thinking like that and working so hard. So karmis are like that. He will eat two capatis or four capatis, but he is working day and night. If you want to see him, he will say, "Oh, I have no time." He does not think at any time that "I am interested to eat four capatis, which are easily available. So why I am working so hard?" But that sense does not come. He is working, working, working, "More money, more money, more money, more money, more money." The Bhagavata says, "No, no. This is not your business." The four capatis is already destined to you; you will get, any circumstances. You don't waste your time simply under some false impression of economic development. Don't waste your time. You cannot get more, you cannot get less. That is already there. So you utilize your time for understanding Krsna. That is your business. People will not accept it. "Oh, this is a waste of time. Attending the class of Bhagavad-gita, this is waste of time. By this time I could have earned hundreds of dollars." That is their business. That is called durbuddhi, durbuddhi, not very intelligent.

~ Srila Prabhupada (Bhagavad-gita 1.23 -- London, July 19, 1973)

12

Modern Slave Camps

Call Centre Workers Limited To Eight Minutes Toilet Time Per Day... And Risk Triggering Alarm If They Go One Second Over

Call centre workers in Norway are protesting against a high-tech surveillance system that triggers an alarm if they spend more than eight minutes per day in the toilet.

Managers are alerted by flashing lights if an employee is away from their desk for a toilet break or other 'personal activities' beyond the allocated time.

But unions and workplace inspectors have branded the practice at insurance company DNB as 'highly intrusive' and a potential breach of their human rights.

Norway's privacy regulator Datatilsynet has now written to DNB telling them the monitoring system is 'a major violation of privacy'.

It said: 'Each individual worker has different needs and these kinds of strict controls deprive the employees of all freedoms over the course of their working day.'

The employees union Finansforbundet described the rules as unacceptable.

A spokesman added: 'Surveying staff to limit toilet visits, cigarette breaks, personal phone calls and other other personal needs to a total of eight minutes per day is highly restrictive and intrusive and must be stopped.'

Career Woman - The Violence of Modern Jobs And The Lost Art of Home Making

Previously in Norway a company ordered all female staff to wear red bracelets during their periods

It is the latest example of 'tyrannical' toilet rules in Norwegian companies.

Last year the country's workplace ombudsman said one firm was reported for making women workers wear a red bracelet when they were having their period to justify more frequent trips to the toilet.

Another company made staff sign a toilet 'visitors book' while a third issued employees with an electronic key card to gain access to the toilets so they could monitor breaks.

Norway's chief workplace ombudsman Bjorn Erik Thon said: 'These are extreme cases of workplace monitoring, but they are real.

'Toilet Codes relating to menstrual cycles are clear violations of privacy and is very insulting to the people concerned.

'We receive many complaints about monitoring in the workplace, which is becoming a growing problem as it is so often being used for something other than what it was originally intended for.

'Wear A Sign When You Want To Use Toilet'

A Spanish factory boss ordered female workers to wear a red sign around their necks when they wanted to use the toilet.

> *Just like here you see in Europe, America. They have got the high standard of life, they have got skyscraper buildings, very big, big roads, motorcars. But what is that? Simply struggling. Are they happy?*
> *—Srila Prabhupada (Lecture, Srimad-Bhagavatam, Vrndavana, December 7, 1975)*

The 400 women staff were told to wear the sign with the word 'aseo' - Spanish for lavatory - written on it in a bid to humiliate them into taking fewer loo-breaks.

Employees at the El Ciruelo fruit packing plant in Murcia even began drinking less water in stifling heat to put off using the toilets.

Humiliating: A female member staff at the Spanish fruit company El Ciruelo in Murcia is shown wearing a sign that reads 'toilet'

This Post Received Thousands Of Comments Which Describe Similar Conditions Prevailing In Other Work Places

This is not a unique situation but a general trend in work places. Some of these comments are reproduced below which confirm the horrors of modern work places.

Remember you are no longer human beings in this world, you are a resource, just like steel, paper, packaging etc. The euphoria of the seventies and the growth of societies that allowed human beings to enjoy life, work and leisure, was swallowed by the accountants and reduced to numbers on a chart

- Andy, Derby, 2/2/2012

Vodafone inbound directory enquiries - 2 minutes toilet break, any longer and you had to explain to manager exactly why. I was very ill following a miscarriage and the manager came looking for me to see why I'd been over 2 minutes. Human rights? Pah!

- Mamastar, 1/2/2012

British Airways call centre, Manchester.. It's a "Bio-break" there with the managers screens going red after 7 minutes absence during the course of the day! Worst job I ever had.

- JoeyR, Leeds, Manchester UK, 1/2/2012

And how much loyalty can you expect slaves to show to their masters? Just a thought...
- DrMallard, West Palm Beach, Florida, USA, 1/2/2012

I worked in a call centre for a while and they tried to stop me from going to the loo one day.......I said "That's fine..no problem at all" then I just ended up peeing on the floor when finally couldn't control...
- Sara, London, 1/2/2012

This type of employer restriction used to be against the law. A deliberate policy to restrict the natural needs of workers. What a nasty sweat shop of a country we have become.

People are not happy actually. Now, so far materialistic happiness is concerned, your country, America, is number one. You are all qualified boys and girls, I see. But still, if we calculate impartially, what is the advantage? The advantage: hand to mouth. You earn in the morning and eat in the evening -- finished. You see? Such qualified boys that... I take, for example, Gaurasundara. He is thoughtful. He is educated. He knows so many things, artist. But for livelihood he has to go early in the morning and come late in the evening. So what is the result? This is the way of materialistic life. Life means that they should not work. Working hard, very hard working, that is the animal's business. The animal should be engaged to work hard for feeding, whole day. Just like the cow is standing here, sometimes eating this, sometime eating that, sometime eating that. What is the business? Only business: to fill up the belly. That's all. But after all qualification, if one has to do the same thing just to fill up the belly, working twelve hours, fourteen hours, then what is this civilization? Has this civilization given the opportunity that "Oh, you have no more to work. Simply sit down, every, all comforts." You can say some of the rich men, they are employing like that, but they are enjoying at the cost of others. They have made such machinery that hundreds of men will work for them and they will sit down and enjoy. What is the enjoyment? Women and wine. That's all. Therefore some, a section of people, revolting-Communists.

So this materialistic way of life is not human life. It is less than animal life. Animal also does not work so hard. You see? And the people are engaged,

(Cont. on the next page....)

- Sylvia, Northumberland, 1/2/2012

Working for a company doing inbound directory Enquiries, we had to complete each call within 25 secs and as soon as you got off one call within 1 second you was on the next call, all time was monitored, including toilet breaks. At the end of my shift I had fried brains. Now the government want to put sick people into these kinds of stressful jobs.

- John.mitch, Belfast, 1/2/2012

This is what happens when profit is put before people and an organisation is run by anti-humans, obsessed with targets and costs. How desperately sad, but everyone in the know knows this kind of thing is normal in the UK too. Maybe not the red bracelets though...yet.

- Deborah, 1/2/2012

> (....Cont. from the previous page)
> wherever you go, the very big highways. What is called? Freeways. Four lines of motor cars running this way and four lines of motor cars running this way at the speed of seventy miles, and everyone is busy. You see? And they take, "It is a very good civilization." And if you shortcut your hard labor, sit down and discuss what is the Absolute Truth, what is the philosophy of life, "They are nonsense." You see? And if you work day and night, hard labor, and to get that energy, inject some medicine or some tranquilizer and this and that... You see? This is the..., going on. So actually, this is not life. This is cats' and dogs' life. That is the verdict of Srimad-Bhagavatam. Nayam deho deha-bhajam nr-loke kastan kaman arhate vid-bhujam ye: [SB 5.5.1] "This life, human form of life, is not meant for working so hard just like animals." Then? "This kind of engagement is for the dogs and hogs." The hogs also, they work the whole day and night and have some sex pleasure. They are happy. So is that life, simply working day and night hard and enjoy some sex pleasure some way or other, and we are thinking happy? No. This is not life. Life is to utilize the energy for perpetual happiness. They do not know that there is some perpetual happiness, there is perpetual life.
>
> ~ Srila Prabhupada (Lecture, Srimad-Bhagavatam 7.9.8 -- Hawaii, March 21, 1969)

I fail to see how this is breaking news. Egg bank were doing this 10 years ago!!
- Julie Watts, Derby, UK, 1/2/2012

Working in a call centre is a fast track to mental illness. Ask anyone who has worked in one.
- Richard, Yorkshire, 1/2/2012

I've worked at call centres for BT, and for a major software company. Both did the same thing - if you wanted to go to the toilet, you were given a code which you had to put in your phone, and if you went over your allotted time your manager wanted to know why. Worse, at the software company a report went to the whole team each day so that each person could 'see where they went wrong' and coincidentally also see how much time their colleagues spent on the toilet...
- Christy Andersen, Newcastle, UK, 1/2/2012

Its not unique to Norway. Lets concentrate on our own country!
- Cat, Midlands, 1/2/2012

And we criticize the Chinese how absolutely hypercritical can you get? - Carl Barron, Christchurch, Dorset,

So too bad for people who suffer from IBS or some other gastrointestinal complaint! too bad for the women who have to visit the loo at that time of the month! too bad for the worker with gas buildup...guess the co-workers will just have to put up with the smell! Honestly, people are not treated as a human these days! Workers are adults, who should be able to determine what amount of time and frequency they need to attend to normal bodily functions. Just typing this, i think i have passed wind at least 5 times and made one trip to the loo for no 1's...if i was working in that company, i guess i wouldn't be too popular tonight!
- Blondie, Wales, 1/2/2012

Same thing happens within BT Openreach repair centres......

- Matt Munro, Bristol, UK, 1/2/2012

I used to work in a a large mail order company, they were the same, however there was no union so they got away with it... It's shocking really, we should name and shame... Next.
- Laura, Oz, 1/2/2012

What are you supposed to do if you have a dose of diarrhoea?
- Honest joe, 1/2/2012

This is why I quit my job in a call centre. It was incredibly stressful. The more recent one I tried was very difficult for me. I found that with the constant talking, my mouth got incredibly dry, hence the need to drink more, hence the need to go to the loo more. I have made a clear decision that this is not the right work environment for me. I did not enjoy being treated as a recalcitrant child. I used to go home depressed at the end of the day. I was consumed by this job and it was so draining. Well the supervisor rang me up to ask me why I was not taking any calls. I am currently upskilling so that I can make a change into something more appropriate.
- RLH, Sydney, Australia, 1/2/2012

When I worked at NHS Direct we were monitored similarly. Needless to say a lot of us left.
- Chloe, UK, 1/2/2012

I wonder does that include travelling time to and from the toilet?
- Paul, Surrey, 1/2/2012

Every night I still hear my former team leader shout that dreaded phrase .... CALLS WAITING!!!

"Innocent men, women, they are kept in that factory simply for livelihood. A little work will provide their needs. Nature has given so much facility. They can grow a little food anywhere. The cows are there in the pasturing ground. Take milk and live peacefully. Why you open factories?"
— *Srila Prabhupada (New Vrindavan, June 26, 1976)*

Career Woman - The Violence of Modern Jobs And The Lost Art of Home Making

- Dagenham Dave, London, 1/2/2012 0:38

Errr...since when is this news??? I work in a call centre for a major bank, in an eight hour shift we are allowed 14 minutes 'productivity' time. We can split this up during the day for loo breaks, getting a drink etc. But if we are even a few seconds over it, the next day you get an interrogation from your manager and have to explain why you are over the time. I am in mid 30s and have two children and don't mind saying that I need to p** at least a few times a day! Come 5pm I am literally running out the door before I explode =(And its hard enough when every single customer thinks It's my personal fault that the tax payer had to bail us out and that our chief exec gets a bazillion pound bonus! The abuse is unbelieveable at times. Anyway, needs must, bills have to get paid so I put up with it and dream of the day when I can finally tell them to shove it. Now where did I put that lottery ticket..........

- Jena, Glasgow, 1/2/2012

I worked in a call centre. On my break on my last day I went out and bought cakes for everyone and was 5 minutes late back from my break (in my 2 years there, my time keeping was impeccable). During my exit interview held 1 hour before I left for the last time ever, the manager gave me a warning because I had been late from my break!! I promised her I wouldn't do it again....

- - Al, Warrington, 1/2/2012

About forty years ago I was working as a storeman in a paintbrush factory, I received an emergency call from a hospital saying my

> *They are thinking: "Advancement of civilization." Advancement of civilization means "Exploit others and you become happy." This is advancement of civilization. "Others may die for such, out of starvation, and one man takes all the money and spends it for wine and women and motor car." That's all. This is advancement of civilization. Sarve sukhino bhavantu. This is Vedic civilization. "Let everyone be happy." That is Vedic civilization. And the demonic civilization, they're: "Let everyone suffer; I become happy. That's all."*
>
> ~ *Srila Prabhupada (Morning Walk -- March 15, 1974, Vrndavana)*

grandmother was close to death, I was told I could not leave until a workmate returned from a dental appointment. I was told that if I left before this I would have no job to return to, I finally got to the hospital less than half an hour before my grandmother died.

- Nick M, Birmingham UK, 1/2/2012

In this country NHS Direct call handlers and nurses have been monitored on toilet (comfort) breaks for years.

- Gideon Webley, Wakefield, 31/1/2012

I saw workers being treated in a very similar way back in England when I was working at an award winning international company. It's not just call centres though - as a student I worked in a major high street department store. You were expected not to go to the bathroom or have a drink during a 4 hour shift chunk. Not very handy for certain times of the month!! If you did need to go, you had to find the head of department and get permission like a school kid, and it was marked down like a crime in 'the book'! It was a huge store with loads of staff per department so it wasn't like it caused a problem.

- JJ, expat, Canada (will return when the government represents its people), 31/1/2012

Try having IBS mate, you can be on the toilet for 30 mins in excruciating pain being literally held hostage by your bowels when all you want is to have a normal working day. I have worked in a sompany and they made you press a 'time out' button on your computer which flashed up a big timer to show how long you'd been away from your desk (which the supervisors would come and check). It's humiliating and embarrassing, people shouldn't be punished for things they can't help and have no control over, especially when there's no cure! These places are the pits, and it's bad enough for people who have normal bodily processes. Since leaving (fortunately just paying my way through university) I know how mind numbing and horrible it is to work in them!

- Marcus, London, 31/1/2012

Career Woman - The Violence of Modern Jobs And The Lost Art of Home Making

Source
Ian Sparks, The Daily Mail, 31 January 2012
http://www.labourstart.org/2013
Where Is Everyone? Attrition Rates In Call Centres, August 31, 2013, The Secret Diary of A Call Centre

Of course, in our India, Hindu conception of life, a woman is always protected. She is protected during her childhood by the father, and she is protected in her youth by the husband, and she is protected in her old age by her sons. That is the conception. And the woman, the cow, the brahmana, the children -- they are meant for absolute protection. That is the Vedic conception. They should always be given full protection. The children, the women, the brahmanas, and the cows, they have no fault. In the laws of the state, a woman, a child, a brahmana and cow has no fault. In the criminal court they are never prosecuted. That is the Hindu law.

~ Srila Prabhupada (Bhagavad-gita Lecture, 2.44-45, 2.58 -- New York, March 25, 1966)

13

Why Women Leave Tech

It's The Slavery, Not Because 'Math Is Hard'

By Kieran Snyder

This is a summary of stories from 716 women who left tech show that the industry's culture is the primary culprit, not any issues related to science education.

I knew something was up when Sandhya, a talented project manager I only knew slightly, asked me if we could have lunch.

She had recently come back from maternity leave. In her note, she said she wanted some advice from another mom.

Over lunch, she confided in me that she was thinking of quitting. It was too hard to juggle everything. Her manager had pressured her to return from leave early, and was pushing her again to take a business trip and leave her nursing infant at home. She wasn't sleeping. She felt like she was failing her job and her child at the same time.

I assured her that her feelings were normal and that much of it would pass. I encouraged her to say no to her manager. I offered to speak to him on her behalf. Although she earned more than her husband did, she quit two weeks later.

That was four years ago, and Sandhya still hasn't returned to the tech industry. She has no plans to. She has since had another baby.

Her story has haunted me since. She came looking for support, and I felt like I failed her.

Over the last month, I have collected stories from 716 other women who have left the tech industry. Their average tenure in the industry was a little over seven years. All of them shared their single biggest reason for leaving, their current employment status, and their desire (or not) to return to tech.

Motherhood As Just The Final Push

Like many of the women I surveyed, Annabelle is highly educated; she has a PhD in linguistics and a master's degree in computer science. She is one of 484 women to cite motherhood as a factor in her decision to leave tech. Unlike the 42 women who

said they wanted to be stay-at-home mothers, Annabelle's decision to leave was not planned:

"I was the first and only person at my small company ever to take maternity leave. They had no parental leave policy previously even though they had been around for about a decade, and, having under 50 employees, weren't covered by FMLA (Family and Medical Leave Act). I (cluelessly!) agreed to go back to work part-time starting when my daughter was six weeks. There was no set place for me to pump [breast milk] while I was at work, so it was perpetually inconvenient and awkward to work at the office for longer than a couple hours at a time."

Eighty-five women cited maternity leave policy as a major factor in their decision to leave their tech jobs. That's over 10% of the women I surveyed. Caitlin, who worked as a data center developer for over a decade, said the following:

"I negotiated 12 unpaid weeks off when my son was born. Only it wasn't really time off. I didn't have to go to the office every day, but I was expected to maintain regular beeper duties and respond within 15 minutes any time there was a problem. I'd be nursing my screaming baby and freaking out that I was going to get fired if I didn't answer the beeping thing right away."

Many women said that it wasn't motherhood alone that did in their careers. Rather, it was the lack of flexible work arrangements,

> But here in this material world they are engaged in very, very hard work. They have invented so many factories, iron factories, melting the iron, these machinery, and it is called ugra karma, asuric karma. After all, you will eat some bread and some fruit or some flower. Why you have invented so big, big factories? That is avidya, nescience, avidya. Suppose hundred years ago there was no factory. So all the people of the world were starving? Eh? Nobody was staring. In, in, in our Vedic literature we don't find any mention anywhere about the factory. No. There is no mention. And how opulent they were. Even in Vrndavana. In Vrndavana, as soon as Kamsa invited Nanda Maharaja, immediately they took wagons of milk preparation to distribute. And you will find in the literature they are all well dressed, well fed. They have got enough food, enough milk, enough cows. But they are village, village men. Vrndavana is a village. There is no scarcity. No moroseness, always jolly, dancing, chanting and eating. So we have created these problems. Simply you have created. Now, you have created so many horseless carriages, now the problem is where to get petrol. In your country it has become a problem. Brahmananda was speaking to me yesterday. There are so many problems. Simply unnecessarily we have created so many artificial wants. Kama-karmabhih.
>
> ~ Srila Prabhupada (Srimad-Bhagavatam 1.8.35 -- Los Angeles, April 27, 1973)

the unsupportive work environment, or a salary that was inadequate to pay for childcare. As Rebecca, a former motion graphics designer, put it, "Motherhood was just the amplifier. It made all the problems that I'd been putting up with forever actually intolerable."

"Everyone's the same, and no one's like me."

One-hundred-ninety-two women cited discomfort working in environments that felt overtly or implicitly discriminatory as a primary factor in their decision to leave tech. That's just over a quarter of the women surveyed. Several of them mention discrimination related to their age, race, or sexuality in addition to gender and motherhood. Dinah was a front-end developer for eight years before deciding to call it quits:

"Literally 28 of the 30 people in our company were white, straight men under 35. I was the only woman. I was one of only two gay people. I was the only person of color other than one guy from Japan. My coworkers called me Halle Berry. As in, 'Oh look, Halle Berry broke the website today.' I'm pretty sure for some of them I'm the only actual black person they've ever spoken to. Everyone was the same, and no one was like me. How could I stay in that situation?"

Never Going Back

Of the 716 women surveyed, 465 are not working today. Two-hundred-fifty-one are employed in non-tech jobs, and 45 of those are running their own companies. A whopping 625 women say they have no plans to return to tech. Only 22—that's 3%—say they would definitely like to.

Stella, a senior leader with almost 20 years of experience in engineering, talks about her experience quitting and starting an ecotourism travel company:

"I love coding. I have a masters in CS [computer science]. I worked in tech for two decades. So many women like me, so highly trained and for what? It was hard enough being the only woman on most projects. Try being the only woman over 40. Doesn't matter how good you are, or even if your colleagues respect you. Eventually you get tired of being the odd duck. I took all my experience and started my own thing where I could make the rules. I'm never going back."

The Pipeline Isn't The Problem

It is popular to characterize the gender gap in tech in terms of a pipeline problem: not enough girls studying math and science. However, there are several indications that this may no longer be the case, at least not to the extent that it once was. High school girls and boys participate about equally in STEM electives (Science, Technology, Engineering and Math). Elite institutions like Stanford and Berkeley now report that about 50% of their introductory computer science students are women. Yet just last year, the U.S. Census Bureau reported that men are employed in STEM occupations at about twice the rate of women with the same qualifications.

Almost everyone I spoke with said that they had enjoyed the work itself. Most mothers added that they would have happily returned to their jobs a few months after giving birth, but their companies didn't offer maternity leave and they needed to quit in order to have their kids. Some women felt that their work environments were discriminatory, but most reported something milder: the simple discomfort of not fitting in in an otherwise homogenous setting. It

Rising Economic Insecurity among Senior Single Women (October 2011). Nearly half (47%) of all senior single women in America do not have adequate retirement resources to meet even their most basic needs for the remainder of their lives, and this number is rising. This distressing statistic is among the findings from a report released by IASP and Dēmos, the latest in the Living Longer on Less series. This report finds that rising housing expenses, fixed and inadequate household budgets, and very low levels of retirement assets are contributing to rapidly rising economic insecurity among senior single women. Single women are especially vulnerable to economic insecurity in retirement due to the limited lifetime asset building capacity many women face, driven by the persistent wage gap, high levels of part-time work and ineligibility for retirement benefits, as well as extended periods out of the labor force due to family care-giving duties.

~ National Council on Aging (NCOA)

may not sound like a big deal if you're used to being in the majority, but it was enough to drive many qualified engineers to quit.

There may be work to do on the pipeline, but the pipeline isn't the problem. Women are leaving tech because they're unhappy with the work environment, not because they have lost interest in the work.

As cultural issues go, this is an incredibly expensive problem. Like my friend Sandhya, these women are educated, highly trained, and weren't planning to quit. We're losing them anyway. And once we've lost them, we almost never get them back.

Source:
Kieran Snyder, The Fortune, October 2, 2014

However, this has not improved the social condition of the world. Actually, a woman should be given protection at every stage of life. She should be given protection by the father in her younger days, by the husband in her youth, and by the grown-up sons in her old age. This is proper social behavior according to the Manu-samhita. But modern education has artificially devised a puffed -- up concept of womanly life, and therefore marriage is practically now an imagination in human society. The social condition of women is thus not very good now, although those who are married are in a better condition than those who are proclaiming their so-called freedom. The demons, therefore, do not accept any instruction which is good for society, and because they do not follow the experience of great sages and the rules and regulations laid down by the sages, the social condition of the demoniac people is very miserable.

~ Srila Prabhupada (Bhagavad-gita 16.7 purport)

14

Soaring Number Of Career Women

'Killed By Alcohol' And Figure Is Rising Faster Than Men

A UK Case Study

The number of alcohol-related deaths among career women has soared over the past decade and is now rising faster than among men, figures reveal.

For women in high-flying roles such as chief executives, doctors and lawyers, the number of deaths caused by drinking has risen by 23 per cent in UK.

And at lower management level, those losing their lives to liver disease and other conditions caused by alcohol rose by 17 per cent.

Among men, the number of deaths in both categories were higher but rose less sharply – the toll for 2011 was 15 per cent higher than in 2001.

The rising deaths are just the 'tip of the iceberg' when it comes to measuring the total damage to the nation's health caused by alcohol.

Harmful drinking among middle-class and middle-aged women is also fuelling rising rates of liver disease, cancer and high blood pressure, which can cause strokes and heart attacks.

Tory MP Tracey Crouch, chairman of the All-party Group on Alcohol Misuse, said: 'A harmful drinker is drinking more than 35 units a week. That's the equivalent of half a bottle of wine a night.

'A lot of people drink far more units than they realise, especially women. I think there are a whole combination of reasons – it's become more socially acceptable, the availability and low cost of wine *and the pressures on professional women when you are working and also have a house to run.*

'We need to look at education and raising awareness about this at the workplace.'

Among women, deaths caused by alcohol poisoning, liver disease, hepatitis or alcohol-related heart and pancreas failure saw a 20 per cent rise in last one decade.

For women in 'higher professional' occupations, rate of rise in deaths was the same.

In 'intermediate occupations', such as secretarial or other skilled office work, it rose by 47 per cent – according to data for England and Wales from a Freedom of Information request to the Office for National Statistics.

For women in low-skilled and technical jobs deaths from alcohol has remained the same since 2001. For 'semi routine' jobs such as shop assistants and hair dressers, it has risen 47 per cent.

In men deaths from alcohol rose by 22 per cent over a decade, of which the highest toll was among those in manual jobs.

One unit of alcohol is around half a glass of wine. According to the doctors, women are recommended to drink no more than 14 units a week, while for men the figure is 21

Research last year showed that middle-aged professional women are drinking more alcohol than teenagers for the first time. Over-55s drink more than any other age group and are now the biggest burden on the NHS (National Health Service).

Professor Ian Gilmore, chair of the UK Alcohol Health Alliance, said rates of almost all serious diseases in the young and middle-aged have fallen as we live longer, but liver disease is rising 'dramatically'.

He said: 'These figures are just the tip of the iceberg, as they are the cases where alcohol is specifically mentioned on the death certificate.

'When you look at diseases where alcohol is a major factor, such as oesophageal and throat cancer, or strokes, the true toll is much larger. When I became a liver consultant 30 years ago, to see a woman dying with alcohol-related liver disease was really rare.

'Today it's not common, but every liver specialist will have seen women in their late 20s or early 30s dying of alcoholic liver disease.'

Professor Gilmore backs the Government's planned introduction of a minimum alcohol price per unit.

He argues research shows the price of alcohol has a major effect on drinking in every social class.

Emily Robinson, director of campaigns at Alcohol Concern, said: 'An increasing number of middle-class, professional women are drinking over safe limits and figures show they drink twice the amount of women in manual jobs.

'If we're to tackle this, it's crucial that workplaces take this issue seriously which is why we've raised the issue with a group of MPs.'

Alcohol Increases Suicide Risk Among Women

Alcohol use increases suicide risk among women, especially those who have symptoms of insomnia such as sleep disturbance and daytime tiredness, shows research.

"These results are important as they help demonstrate that alcohol use is associated with an increase in suicide risk, and that this increase may be partially due to insomnia symptoms," says principal investigator Michael Nadorff, assistant professor at Mississippi State University.

The study suggests that the targeted assessment and treatment of specific sleep problems may reduce the risk of suicide among those who consume alcohol. "By better understanding this relationship, and the mechanisms associated with increased risk, we can better design interventions to reduce suicide risk," Nadorff adds.

The study involved 375 undergraduate students at an university in the US.

The participants completed an online questionnaire that examined insomnia symptoms, nightmares, alcohol use and suicide risk.

If young boys and young girls mix freely and have sex, and as soon as she is pregnant, you go away, let her suffer, no responsibility. The poor girl, long before, father, mother divorce -- no protector. And as soon as she selects somebody husband, and as soon as pregnancy, he goes away. And old age -- there is no family, no son. Ninety-nine percent the woman class live like that. How hopelessly the old ladies are sitting down -- only one cat, one dog, one television. The old men also like that, hopelessness. Or drinking or seeing the television. And a dog friend. Is that life?

~ Srila Prabhupada (Room Conversation -- January 26, 1977, Puri)

The study appeared in the Journal of Clinical Sleep Medicine.

Source:
Tamara Cohen, The Daily Mail, 25 January 2013
IANS, Hindustan Times, December 24, 2014

15

It Takes A Village To Raise A Child

No Mom Is an Island

If you're like most moms, while you're reading this you're probably cooking dinner, wiping noses, paying bills, juggling dishes, checking homework, and working an extra job -- all with the phone wedged between your ear and shoulder as you're asking your mom about her back pain.

When you think of what the average mother packs into 24 hours, it's no wonder so many feel just one little wobbly, baby-step away from... total collapse!

Yet, many overworked moms and dads have trouble reaching out for help. They think they're supposed to manage all their family responsibilities on their own. But, is that right... or a big lie? When did having a doula or baby sitter become a sign of being soft and self-indulgent? When did it become taboo to ask for help?

In truth, all parents need support. That's why the ancient adage, "It takes a village to raise a child," has stuck over the years. Whether you live in Turkey or Trinidad -- caring for a child actually does take a village!

Throughout history, parents have always had lots of help: The old-fashioned, hands-on support team of grandparents, aunts, cousins, older siblings, and neighbors -- who lived close by, if not right in the house with us. We could just drop the kids off at the next-door neighbor's for a few hours (even without calling up ahead of time). And, instead of surfing the Web for parenting advice, we'd simply turn to family and friends... society's original search engine.

But about 50 years ago, our parent support team began to unravel putting moms and dads under increasing stress. Increasingly, the neighbors are too busy working to help us, good baby-sitters are hard to find, and our families are spread far and wide.

Added to this burden, modern moms have the unhappy distinction (along with moms in Liberia and New Guinea) of living in the only nations without mandatory paid maternity leave to allow them a protected time to nurture their newborns before heading back to the office or factory.

Furthermore, although today's parents may be the most educated in history, they may also be the least experienced when it comes to caring for young children. That means they need lots of information and counsel. Many new parents have never even held an infant before giving birth to their own. (Some feel so unready; they imagine that a shoplifting alarm might suddenly blare when they walk out of the hospital with their new baby!)

So, in order for families to thrive, parents need to reject the myth that asking for help is an extravagance or a sign of weakness. Far from indicating failure, it's actually a sign of courage and strength.

And, when parents ask others for help they actually give their community a chance to help itself because raising happy, healthy children strengthens the entire society.

This is perfectly understood by the Masai of East Africa. When they greet each other, they don't ask "How's business?" or even "How are you?" They ask, "How are the children?" And the correct response is: "All the children are fine." They say, "All the children!" because even these fierce warriors understand that each person must

---

Prabhupada: Now these rascal Westerners, there the women claiming equal rights. Change that the man will give birth to a child and not the woman. Equal rights. Make agreement. "Once you beget; once I shall." Make this contract. Then it is equal right. If the woman has to give birth of a child and she has to suffer all the pains thereof, then where is the equal right? Where is equal right? Nature has said, "You must suffer." The husband, the so-called husband, will utilize you for sex satisfaction, and you will be pregnant, and he will go away and you will suffer whole life to maintain the child, welfare -- "Give me some money" -- or this or that. Where is equal right? He is free. He has gone away. Huh? This is general experience in the Western countries.

Brahmananda: "Unwed mothers."

Prabhupada: Yes. And she cannot also check that "I shall not become mother." For sex appetite she will agree, and the man will go away and she will suffer. Is that civilization?

Brahmananda: Each year there are over one million abortions in America.

Prabhupada: And they are advanced. They are proud of their being advanced. And they will not suffer? So we are trying to save the whole human society from rascaldom. That's all. This is Krsna consciousness. You see? If they kindly accept and follow this movement they will be happy. Otherwise they are doomed. Let them suffer. What can I do? Thorough overhauling required.

~ Srila Prabhupada (Morning Walk -- September 25, 1975, Ahmedabad)

be concerned about the nurturing and protection of all children in order to strengthen the community and create a better future for the entire group.

So go ahead and ask for help. Ask a friend to bring over a casserole or ask another mom to watch your tot when you have to work late (and offer to watch hers for a few hours in return). You may be surprised at how willing friends and family are to pitch in.

And, when today's hectic world has you feeling overwhelmed, slow down, and let go of the idea that everything has to be perfect. Take a breath, laugh at how silly life is and take the time to focus on what is most important, your child's needs... and your health and sanity!

And, most importantly, remember that no mom is an island unto herself. Seeking help from your own personal village is not only fine, it's one of the smartest things any mother can do.

Source
Harvey Karp, No Mom Is an Island
The Huffington Post, 19/01/2012

16

Why Women Still Can't Have It All

By Anne-Marie Slaughterjun

It's time to stop fooling ourselves, says a woman who left a position of power: the women who have managed to be both mothers and top professionals are superhuman, rich, or self-employed. If we truly believe in equal opportunity for all women, here's what has to change.

Eighteen months into my job as the first woman director of policy planning at the State Department, a foreign-policy dream job that traces its origins back to George Kennan, I found myself in New York, at the United Nations' annual assemblage of every foreign minister and head of state in the world. On a Wednesday evening, President and Mrs. Obama hosted a glamorous reception at the American Museum of Natural History. I sipped champagne, greeted foreign dignitaries, and mingled. But I could not stop thinking about my 14-year-old son, who had started eighth grade three weeks earlier and was already resuming what had become his

pattern of skipping homework, disrupting classes, failing math, and tuning out any adult who tried to reach him.

Over the summer, we had barely spoken to each other—or, more accurately, he had barely spoken to me. And the previous spring I had received several urgent phone calls—invariably on the day of an important meeting—that required me to take the first train from Washington, D.C., where I worked, back to Princeton, New Jersey, where he lived. My husband, who has always done everything possible to support my career, took care of him and his 12-year-old brother during the week; outside of those midweek emergencies, I came home only on weekends.

As the evening wore on, I ran into a colleague who held a senior position in the White House. She has two sons exactly my sons' ages, but she had chosen to move them from California to D.C. when she got her job, which meant her husband commuted back to California regularly. I told her how difficult I was finding it to be away from my son when he clearly needed me. Then I said, "When this is over, I'm going to write an op-ed titled 'Women Can't Have It All.'"

A High Profile Career Woman Can't Write That

She was horrified. "You can't write that," she said. "You, of all people." What she meant was that such a statement, coming from a high-profile career woman—a role model—would be a terrible

signal to younger generations of women. By the end of the evening, she had talked me out of it, but for the remainder of my stint in Washington, I was increasingly aware that the feminist beliefs on which I had built my entire career were shifting under my feet. I had always assumed that if I could get a foreign-policy job in the State Department or the White House while my party was in power, I would stay the course as long as I had the opportunity to do the work I loved. But in January 2011, when my two-year public-service leave from Princeton University was up, I hurried home as fast as I could.

Hurrying Home

A rude epiphany hit me soon after I got there. When people asked why I had left government, I explained that I'd come home not only because of Princeton's rules (after two years of leave, you lose your tenure), but also because of my desire to be with my family and my conclusion that juggling high-level government work with the needs of two teenage boys was not possible. I have not exactly left the ranks of full-time career women: I teach a full course load; write regular print and online columns on foreign policy; give 40 to 50 speeches a year; appear regularly on TV and radio; and am working on a new academic book. But I routinely got reactions from other women my age or older that ranged from disappointed ("It's such a pity that you had to leave Washington") to condescending ("I wouldn't generalize from your experience. I've never had to compromise, and my kids turned out great").

The first set of reactions, with the underlying assumption that my choice was somehow sad or unfortunate, was irksome enough. But it was the second set of reactions—those implying that my parenting and/or my commitment to my profession were somehow substandard—that triggered a blind fury. Suddenly, finally, the penny dropped. All my life, I'd been on the other side of this exchange. I'd been the woman smiling the faintly superior smile while another woman told me she had decided to take some time out or pursue a less competitive career track so that she could spend more time with her family. I'd been the woman congratulating herself on her unswerving commitment to the feminist cause, chatting smugly with her dwindling number of college or law-school friends who had reached and maintained their place on the highest rungs of their profession. I'd been the one telling young women at my lectures that you can have it all and do it all, regardless of what field you are in. Which means I'd been part, albeit unwittingly, of making millions of women feel that they are to blame if they cannot manage to rise up the ladder as fast as men and also have a family and an active home life (and be thin and beautiful to boot).

You Can Have It All - But Not Today, Not With The Way Our Economy And Society Are Currently Structured

Last spring, I flew to Oxford to give a public lecture. At the request of a young Rhodes Scholar I know, I'd agreed to talk to the Rhodes community about "work-family balance." I ended up speaking to a group of about 40 men and women in their mid-20s.

What poured out of me was a set of very frank reflections on how unexpectedly hard it was to do the kind of job I wanted to do as a high government official and be the kind of parent I wanted to be, at a demanding time for my children (even though my husband, an academic, was willing to take on the lion's share of parenting for the two years I was in Washington).

I concluded by saying that my time in office had convinced me that further government service would be very unlikely while my sons were still at home. The audience was rapt, and asked many thoughtful questions. One of the first was from a young woman who began by thanking me for "not giving just one more fatuous 'You can have it all' talk." Just about all of the women in that room planned to combine careers and family in some way. But almost all assumed and accepted that they would have to make compromises that the men in their lives were far less likely to have to make.

The striking gap between the responses I heard from those young women (and others like them) and the responses I heard from my peers and associates prompted me to write this article. Women of my generation have clung to the feminist credo we were raised with, even as our ranks have been steadily thinned by unresolvable tensions between family and career, because we are determined not to drop the flag for the next generation. But when many members of the younger generation have stopped listening, on the grounds that glibly repeating "you can have it all" is simply airbrushing reality, it is time to talk.

I still strongly believe that women can "have it all" (and that men can too). I believe that we can "have it all at the same time." But not today, not with the way America's economy and society are currently structured. My experiences over the past three years have forced me to confront a number of uncomfortable facts that need to be widely acknowledged—and quickly changed.

I Could No Longer Be Both The Parent And The Professional

Before my service in government, I'd spent my career in academia: as a law professor and then as the dean of Princeton's Woodrow Wilson School of Public and International Affairs. Both were demanding jobs, but I had the ability to set my own schedule most of the time. I could be with my kids when I needed to be, and still get the work done. I had to travel frequently, but I found I could make up for that with an extended period at home or a family vacation.

"When I want to watch a realistic comedy about a working mom, I'll look in the mirror."

I knew that I was lucky in my career choice, but I had no idea how lucky until I spent two years in Washington within a rigid bureaucracy, even with bosses as understanding as Hillary Clinton and her chief of staff, Cheryl Mills.

My workweek started at 4:20 on Monday morning, when I got up to get the 5:30 train from Trenton to Washington. It ended late on Friday, with the train home. In between, the days were crammed with meetings, and when the meetings stopped, the writing work began—a never-ending stream of memos, reports, and comments on other people's drafts. For two years, I never left the office early enough to go to any stores other than those open 24 hours, which meant that everything from dry cleaning to hair appointments to Christmas shopping had to be done on weekends, amid children's sporting events, music lessons, family meals, and conference calls.

I was entitled to four hours of vacation per pay period, which came to one day of vacation a month. And I had it better than many of my peers in D.C.; Secretary Clinton deliberately came in around 8 a.m. and left around 7 p.m., to allow her close staff to have morning and evening time with their families (although of course she worked earlier and later, from home).

In short, the minute I found myself in a job that is typical for the vast majority of working women (and men), working long hours on someone else's schedule, I could no longer be both the parent and the professional I wanted to be—at least not with a child experiencing a rocky adolescence. I realized what should have perhaps been obvious: having it all, at least for me, depended almost entirely on what type of job I had. The flip side is the harder truth: having it all was not possible in many types of jobs, including high government office—at least not for very long.

Value Family Over Profession

I am hardly alone in this realization. Michèle Flournoy stepped down after three years as undersecretary of defense for policy, the third-highest job in the department, to spend more time at home with her three children, two of whom are teenagers. Karen Hughes left her position as the counselor to President George W. Bush after a year and a half in Washington to go home to Texas for the sake of her family. Mary Matalin, who spent two years as an assistant to Bush and the counselor to Vice President Dick Cheney before stepping down to spend more time with her daughters, wrote: "Having control over your schedule is the only way that women who want to have a career and a family can make it work."

Yet the decision to step down from a position of power—to value family over professional advancement, even for a time—is directly at odds with the prevailing social pressures on career professionals in the United States. One phrase says it all about current attitudes toward work and family, particularly among elites. In Washington, "leaving to spend time with your family" is a euphemism for being fired. This understanding is so ingrained that when Flournoy announced her resignation last December, The New York Times covered her decision as follows:

Ms. Flournoy's announcement surprised friends and a number of Pentagon officials, but all said they took her reason for resignation at face value and not as a standard Washington excuse for an official who has in reality been forced out. "I can absolutely and unequivocally state that her decision to step down has nothing to do with anything

> *After the speech I gave in New York, I went to dinner with a group of 30-somethings. I sat across from two vibrant women, one of whom worked at the UN and the other at a big New York law firm. As nearly always happens in these situations, they soon began asking me about work-life balance. When I told them I was writing this article, the lawyer said, "I look for role models and can't find any." She said the women in her firm who had become partners and taken on management positions had made tremendous sacrifices, "many of which they don't even seem to realize ... They take two years off when their kids are young but then work like crazy to get back on track professionally, which means that they see their kids when they are toddlers but not teenagers, or really barely at all." Her friend nodded, mentioning the top professional women she knew, all of whom essentially relied on round-the-clock nannies. Both were very clear that they did not want that life, but could not figure out how to combine professional success and satisfaction with a real commitment to family.*
>
> ~ *Anne-Marie Slaughterjun*

other than her commitment to her family," said Doug Wilson, a top Pentagon spokesman. "She has loved this job and people here love her."

Think about what this "standard Washington excuse" implies: it is so unthinkable that an official would actually step down to spend time with his or her family that this must be a cover for something else. How could anyone voluntarily leave the circles of power for the responsibilities of parenthood? Depending on one's vantage point, it is either ironic or maddening that this view abides in the nation's capital, despite the ritual commitments to "family values" that are part of every political campaign. Regardless, this sentiment makes true work-life balance exceptionally difficult. But it cannot change unless top women speak out.

Barriers And Flaws In The New Opportunities

I realize that I am blessed to have been born in the late 1950s instead of the early 1930s, as my mother was, or the beginning of the 20th century, as my grandmothers were. My mother built a successful and rewarding career as a professional artist largely in the years after my brothers and I left home—and after being told in her 20s that she could not go to medical school, as her father had done and her brother would go on to do, because, of course, she was going to get married. I owe my own freedoms and opportunities to the pioneering generation of women ahead of me—the women now in their 60s, 70s, and 80s who faced overt sexism of a kind I see only when watching Mad Men, and who knew that the only way to make it as a woman was to act exactly like a man. To admit to, much less act on, maternal longings would have been fatal to their careers.

But precisely thanks to their progress, a different kind of conversation is now possible. It is time for women in leadership positions to recognize that although we are still blazing trails and breaking ceilings, many of us are also reinforcing a falsehood: that "having it all" is, more than anything, a function of personal determination. As Kerry Rubin and Lia Macko, the authors of Midlife Crisis at 30, their cri de coeur for Gen-X and Gen-Y women, put it:

What we discovered in our research is that while the empowerment part of the equation has been loudly celebrated, there has been very little honest discussion among women of our age about the real barriers and flaws that still exist in the system despite the opportunities we inherited.

Women Are Less Happy Today Than Their Predecessors

I am well aware that the majority of American women face problems far greater than any discussed in this article. I am writing for my demographic—highly educated, well-off women who are privileged enough to have choices in the first place. *We may not have choices about whether to do paid work, as dual incomes have become indispensable. But we have choices about the type and tempo of the work we do.* We are the women who could be leading, and who should be equally represented in the leadership ranks.

Millions of other working women face much more difficult life circumstances. Some are single mothers; many struggle to find any job; others support husbands who cannot find jobs. Many cope with a work life in which good day care is either unavailable or very expensive; school schedules do not match work schedules; and schools themselves are failing to educate their children.

Many of these women are worrying not about having it all, but rather about holding on to what they do have. And although women as a group have made substantial gains in wages, educational attainment, and prestige over the past three decades, *the economists Justin Wolfers and Betsey Stevenson have shown that women are less happy today than their predecessors were in 1972, both in absolute terms and relative to men.*

The Half-Truths We Hold Dear

Let's briefly examine the stories we tell ourselves, the clichés that I and many other women typically fall back on when younger women ask us how we have managed to "have it all." They are not necessarily lies, but at best partial truths. We must clear them out of the way to make room for a more honest and productive discussion about real solutions to the problems faced by professional women. It's possible if you are just committed enough.

Our usual starting point, whether we say it explicitly or not, is that having it all depends primarily on the depth and intensity of a woman's commitment to her career. That is precisely the sentiment behind the dismay so many older career women feel about the younger generation. They are not committed enough, we say, to make the trade-offs and sacrifices that the women ahead of them made.

Yet instead of chiding, perhaps we should face some basic facts. Very few women reach leadership positions. The pool of female candidates for any top job is small, and will only grow smaller if the women who come after us decide to take time out, or drop out of professional competition altogether, to raise children.

Women Are Not Making It To The Top

That is exactly what has Sheryl Sandberg so upset, and rightly so. In her words, "Women are not making it to the top. A hundred and ninety heads of state; nine are women. Of all the people in parliament in the world, 13 percent are women. In the corporate sector, [the share of] women at the top—C-level jobs, board seats—tops out at 15, 16 percent."

Can "insufficient commitment" even plausibly explain these numbers? To be sure, the women who do make it to the top are highly committed to their profession. On closer examination, however, it turns out that most of them have something else in common: they are genuine superwomen. Consider the number of women recently in the top ranks in Washington—Susan Rice, Elizabeth Sherwood-Randall, Michelle Gavin, Nancy-Ann Min DeParle—who are Rhodes Scholars. Samantha Power, another senior White House official, won a Pulitzer Prize at age 32. Or consider Sandberg herself, who graduated with the prize given to Harvard's top student of economics. These women cannot possibly be the standard against which even very talented professional women should measure themselves. Such a standard sets up most women for a sense of failure.

Those Who Have Made It To The Top

What's more, among those who have made it to the top, a balanced life still is more elusive for women than it is for men. A simple measure is how many women in top positions have children compared with their male colleagues. Every male Supreme Court justice has a family. Two of the three female justices are single with no children. And the third, Ruth Bader Ginsburg, began her career as a judge only when her younger child was almost grown. The pattern is the same at the National Security Council: Condoleezza Rice, the first and only woman national-security adviser, is also the only national-security adviser since the 1950s not to have a family.

"Do you ever worry you've had to sacrifice your femininity to succeed in the male business world."

The line of high-level women appointees in the Obama administration is one woman deep. Virtually all of us who have stepped down have been succeeded by men; searches for women to succeed men in similar positions come up empty. Just about every woman who could plausibly be tapped is already in government.

The rest of the foreign-policy world is not much better; Micah Zenko, a fellow at the Council on Foreign Relations, recently surveyed the best data he could find across the government, the military, the academy, and think tanks, and found that women hold fewer than 30 percent of the senior foreign-policy positions in each of these institutions.

50-50 World Has Not Happened

These numbers are all the more striking when we look back to the 1980s, when women now in their late 40s and 50s were coming out of graduate school, and remember that our classes were nearly 50-50 men and women. We were sure then that by now, we would be living in a 50-50 world. Something derailed that dream.

Sandberg thinks that "something" is an "ambition gap"—that women do not dream big enough. I am all for encouraging young women to reach for the stars. But I fear that the obstacles that keep women from reaching the top are rather more prosaic than the scope of their ambition.

The present system is based on a society that no longer exists—one in which farming was a major occupation and stay-at-home moms were the norm. Yet the system hasn't changed.

Consider some of the responses of women interviewed by Zenko about why "women are significantly underrepresented

'Who says that we never get any credit from men? My boss said that I poured the tea wonderfully today.'

in foreign policy and national security positions in government, academia, and think tanks." Juliette Kayyem, who served as an assistant secretary in the Department of Homeland Security from 2009 to 2011 and now writes a foreign-policy and national-security column for The Boston Globe, told Zenko that among other reasons,

> The basic truth is also this: the travel sucks. As my youngest of three children is now 6, I can look back at the years when they were all young and realize just how disruptive all the travel was. There were also trips I couldn't take because I was pregnant or on leave, the conferences I couldn't attend because (note to conference organizers: weekends are a

bad choice) kids would be home from school, and the various excursions that were offered but just couldn't be managed.

Jolynn Shoemaker, the director of Women in International Security, agreed: "Inflexible schedules, unrelenting travel, and constant pressure to be in the office are common features of these jobs."

These "mundane" issues—the need to travel constantly to succeed, the conflicts between school schedules and work schedules, the insistence that work be done in the office—cannot be solved by exhortations to close the ambition gap. I would hope to see commencement speeches that finger America's social and business policies, rather than women's level of ambition, in explaining the dearth of women at the top. But changing these policies requires much more than speeches. It means fighting the mundane battles—every day, every year—in individual workplaces, in legislatures, and in the media.

Husband - There's My Work-Life Balance.

Sandberg's second message in her Barnard commencement address was: "The most important career decision you're going to make is whether or not you have a life partner and who that partner is." Lisa Jackson, the administrator of the Environmental Protection Agency, recently drove that message home to an audience of Princeton students and alumni gathered to hear her acceptance speech for the James Madison Medal. During the Q&A session, an audience member asked her how she managed her career and her family.

> *Women are very delicate. They should be given protection. It is better for them to remain dependent. That is very good. Independent woman cannot be happy. That's a fact. We have seen in the Western countries, on, in the name of independence, so many women are unhappy. So that is not recommended in the Vedic civilization and in the varnasrama-dharma.*
>
> *~ Srila Prabhupada (Srimad-Bhagavatam 3.25.5-6 -- Bombay, November 5, 1974)*

She laughed and pointed to her husband in the front row, saying: "There's my work-life balance." I could never have had the career I have had without my husband, Andrew Moravcsik, who is a tenured professor of politics and international affairs at Princeton. Andy has spent more time with our sons than I have, not only on homework, but also on baseball, music lessons, photography, card games, and more. When each of them had to bring in a foreign dish for his fourth-grade class dinner, Andy made his grandmother's Hungarian palacsinta; when our older son needed to memorize his lines for a lead role in a school play, he turned to Andy for help.

Still, the proposition that women can have high-powered careers as long as their husbands or partners are willing to share the parenting load equally (or disproportionately) assumes that most women will feel as comfortable as men do about being away from their children, as long as their partner is home with them. In my experience, that is simply not the case.

Family vs. Job - Man vs. Woman

Here I step onto treacherous ground, mined with stereotypes. From years of conversations and observations, however, I've come

to believe that men and women respond quite differently when problems at home force them to recognize that their absence is hurting a child, or at least that their presence would likely help. I do not believe fathers love their children any less than mothers do, but men do seem more likely to choose their job at a cost to their family, while women seem more likely to choose their family at a cost to their job.

Breadwinner vs. Caregiver

Many factors determine this choice, of course. Men are still socialized to believe that their primary family obligation is to be the breadwinner; women, to believe that their primary family obligation is to be the caregiver. But it may be more than that. When I described the choice between my children and my job to Senator Jeanne Shaheen, she said exactly what I felt: "There's really no choice." She wasn't referring to social expectations, but to a maternal imperative felt so deeply that the "choice" is reflexive.

Men and women also seem to frame the choice differently. In Midlife Crisis at 30, Mary Matalin recalls her days working as President Bush's assistant and Vice President Cheney's counselor:

> Even when the stress was overwhelming—those days when I'd cry in the car on the way to work, asking myself "Why am I doing this??"—I always knew the answer to that question: I believe in this president.

Who Needs Me More? Indispensable To My Kids, Not To My Job

But Matalin goes on to describe her choice to leave in words that are again uncannily similar to the explanation I have given so many people since leaving the State Department:

> I finally asked myself, "Who needs me more?" And that's when I realized, it's somebody else's turn to do this job. I'm indispensable to my kids, but I'm not close to indispensable to the White House.

To many men, however, the choice to spend more time with their children, instead of working long hours on issues that affect many lives, seems selfish. Male leaders are routinely praised for having sacrificed their personal life on the altar of public or corporate service. That sacrifice, of course, typically involves their family. Yet their children, too, are trained to value public service over private responsibility.

Society Values More Workers Who Put Their Careers First

At the diplomat Richard Holbrooke's memorial service, one of his sons told the audience that when he was a child, his father was often gone, not around to teach him to throw a ball or to watch his games. But as he grew older, he said, he realized that Holbrooke's absence was the price of saving people around the world—a price worth paying.

It is not clear to me that this ethical framework makes sense for society. Why should we want leaders who fall short on personal responsibilities? Perhaps leaders who invested time in their own families would be more keenly aware of the toll their public choices—on issues from war to welfare—take on private lives. (Kati Marton, Holbrooke's widow and a noted author, says that although Holbrooke adored his children, he came to appreciate the full importance of family only in his 50s, at which point he became a very present parent and grandparent, while continuing to pursue an extraordinary public career.)

Regardless, it is clear which set of choices society values more today. Workers who put their careers first are typically rewarded; workers who choose their families are overlooked, disbelieved, or accused of unprofessionalism.

In sum, having a supportive mate may well be a necessary condition if women are to have it all, but it is not sufficient. If women feel deeply that turning down a promotion that would involve more travel, for instance, is the right thing to do, then they will continue to do that. Ultimately, it is society that must change, coming to value choices to put family ahead of work just as much as those to put work ahead of family. If we really valued those choices, we would value the people who make them; if we valued the people who make them, we would do everything possible to hire and retain them; if we did everything possible to allow them to combine work and family equally over time, then the choices would get a lot easier.

It's Possible If You Sequence It Right.

Young women should be wary of the assertion "You can have it all; you just can't have it all at once." This 21st-century addendum to the original line is now proffered by many senior women to their younger mentees. To the extent that it means, in the words of one working mother, "I'm going to do my best and I'm going to keep the long term in mind and know that it's not always going to be this hard to balance," it is sound advice. But to the extent that it means that women can have it all if they just find the right sequence of career and family, it's cheerfully wrong.

Career First, Kids Later

The most important sequencing issue is when to have children. Many of the top women leaders of the generation just ahead of me—Madeleine Albright, Hillary Clinton, Ruth Bader Ginsburg, Sandra Day O'Connor, Patricia Wald, Nannerl Keohane—had their children in their 20s and early 30s, as was the norm in the 1950s through the 1970s. A child born when his mother is 25 will

"I HAVEN'T DECIDED WHETHER OR NOT I WANT CHILDREN, BUT I KNOW I DON'T WANT ANY HUSBANDS!"

finish high school when his mother is 43, an age at which, with full-time immersion in a career, she still has plenty of time and energy for advancement.

Yet this sequence has fallen out of favor with many high-potential women, and understandably so. People tend to marry later now, and anyway, if you have children earlier, you may have difficulty getting a graduate degree, a good first job, and opportunities for advancement in the crucial early years of your career. Making matters worse, you will also have less income while raising your children, and hence less ability to hire the help that can be indispensable to your juggling act.

When I was the dean, the Woodrow Wilson School created a program called Pathways to Public Service, aimed at advising women whose children were almost grown about how to go into public service, and many women still ask me about the best "on-ramps" to careers in their mid-40s. Honestly, I'm not sure what to tell most of them. Unlike the pioneering women who entered the workforce after having children in the 1970s, these women are competing with their younger selves. Government and NGO jobs are an option, but many careers are effectively closed off. Personally, I have never seen a woman in her 40s enter the academic market successfully, or enter a law firm as a junior associate, Alicia Florrick of The Good Wife notwithstanding.

These considerations are why so many career women of my generation chose to establish themselves in their careers first and have children in their mid-to-late 30s. But that raises the possibility of spending long, stressful years and a small fortune trying to have a baby. I lived that nightmare: for three years, beginning at age 35, I did everything possible to conceive and was frantic at the thought that I had simply left having a biological child until it was too late.

And when everything does work out? I had my first child at 38 (and counted myself blessed) and my second at 40. That means I will be 58 when both of my children are out of the house. What's more, it means that many peak career opportunities are coinciding precisely with their teenage years, when, experienced parents advise, being available as a parent is just as important as in the first years of a child's life.

Try To Have Kids Before You Are 35

Many women of my generation have found themselves, in the prime of their careers, saying no to opportunities they once would have jumped at and hoping those chances come around again later. Many others who have decided to step back for a while, taking on consultant positions or part-time work that lets them spend more time with their children (or aging parents), are worrying about how long they can "stay out" before they lose the competitive edge they worked so hard to acquire.

Given the way our work culture is oriented today, I recommend establishing yourself in your career first but still trying to have kids before you are 35—or else freeze your eggs, whether you are married or not. You may well be a more mature and less frustrated parent in your 30s or 40s; you are also more likely to have found a lasting life partner. But the truth is, neither sequence is optimal, and both involve trade-offs that men do not have to make.

You should be able to have a family if you want one—however and whenever your life circumstances allow—and still have the career you desire. If more women could strike this balance, more women would reach leadership positions. And if more women were

in leadership positions, they could make it easier for more women to stay in the workforce. The rest of this essay details how.

The Culture of "Time Macho"

Back in the Reagan administration, a New York Times story about the ferociously competitive budget director Dick Darman reported, "Mr. Darman sometimes managed to convey the impression that he was the last one working in the Reagan White House by leaving his suit coat on his chair and his office light burning after he left for home." (Darman claimed that it was just easier to leave his suit jacket in the office so he could put it on again in the morning, but his record of psychological manipulation suggests otherwise.)

The culture of "time macho"—a relentless competition to work harder, stay later, pull more all-nighters, travel around the world and bill the extra hours that the international date line affords you—remains astonishingly prevalent among professionals today.

Nothing captures the belief that more time equals more value better than the cult of billable hours afflicting large law firms across the country and providing exactly the wrong incentives for employees who hope to integrate work and family.

Yet even in industries that don't explicitly reward sheer quantity of hours spent on the job, the pressure to arrive early, stay late, and be available, always, for in-person meetings at 11 a.m. on Saturdays can be intense.

Indeed, by some measures, the problem has gotten worse over time: a study by the Center for American Progress reports that nationwide, the share of all professionals—women and men—working more than 50 hours a week has increased since the late 1970s.

"Always On" Mode Of Working

But more time in the office does not always mean more "value added"—and it does not always add up to a more successful organization.

In 2009, Sandra Pocharski, a senior female partner at Monitor Group and the head of the firm's Leadership and Organization practice, commissioned a Harvard Business School professor to assess the factors that helped or hindered women's effectiveness and advancement at Monitor. The study found that the company's culture was characterized by an "always on" mode of working, often without due regard to the impact on employees. Pocharski observed:

> Clients come first, always, and sometimes burning the midnight oil really does make the difference between success and failure. But sometimes we were just defaulting to behavior that overloaded our people without improving results much, if at all. We decided we needed managers to get better at distinguishing between these categories, and to recognize the hidden costs of assuming that "time is cheap." When that time doesn't add a lot of value and comes at a high cost to talented employees, who will leave when the personal cost becomes unsustainable—well, that is clearly a bad outcome for everyone.

I have worked very long hours and pulled plenty of all-nighters myself over the course of my career, including a few nights on my office couch during my two years in D.C.

Being willing to put the time in when the job simply has to get done is rightfully a hallmark of a successful professional. But looking back, I have to admit that my assumption that I would stay late made me much less efficient over the course of the day than I might have been, and certainly less so than some of my colleagues, who managed to get the same amount of work done and go home at a decent hour. If Dick Darman had had a boss who clearly valued prioritization and time management, he might have found reason to turn out the lights and take his jacket home.

Our Work Culture Remains More Office-Centered Than It Needs To Be

Long hours are one thing, and realistically, they are often unavoidable. But do they really need to be spent at the office? To be sure, being in the office some of the time is beneficial. In-person meetings can be far more efficient than phone or e-mail tag; trust and collegiality are much more easily built up around the same physical table; and spontaneous conversations often generate good ideas and lasting relationships. Still, armed with e-mail, instant messaging, phones, and video conferencing technology, we should be able to move to a culture where the office is a base of operations more than the required locus of work.

Being able to work from home—in the evening after children are put to bed, or during their sick days or snow days, and at least some of the time on weekends—can be the key, for mothers, to carrying your full load versus letting a team down at crucial moments. State-of-the-art videoconferencing facilities can dramatically reduce the need for long business trips.

These technologies are making inroads, and allowing easier integration of work and family life. According to the Women's Business Center, 61 percent of women business owners use technology to "integrate the responsibilities of work and home"; 44 percent use technology to allow employees "to work off-site or to have flexible work schedules." Yet our work culture still remains more office-centered than it needs to be, especially in light of technological advances.

One way to change that is by changing the "default rules" that govern office work—the baseline expectations about when, where, and how work will be done.

One real-world example comes from the British Foreign and Commonwealth Office, a place most people are more likely to associate with distinguished gentlemen in pinstripes than with progressive thinking about work-family balance.

Make The Case For Remote Work

Like so many other places, however, the FCO worries about losing talented members of two-career couples around the world, particularly women. So it recently changed its basic policy from a default rule that jobs have to be done on-site to one that assumes that some jobs might be done remotely, and invites workers to make the case for remote work.

Kara Owen, a career foreign-service officer who was the FCO's diversity director and will soon become the British deputy ambassador to France, writes that she has now done two remote jobs. Before her current maternity leave, she was working a London job from Dublin to be with her partner, using teleconferencing technology and timing her trips to London to coincide "with key meetings where I needed to be in the room (or chatting at the pre-meeting coffee) to have an impact, or to do intensive 'network maintenance.'"

In fact, she writes, "I have found the distance and quiet to be a real advantage in a strategic role, providing I have put in the investment up front to develop very strong personal relationships with the game changers." Owen recognizes that not every job can be done this way. But she says that for her part, she has been able to combine family requirements with her career.

Changes in default office rules should not advantage parents over other workers; indeed, done right, they can improve relations among co-workers by raising their awareness of each other's circumstances and instilling a sense of fairness.

Two years ago, the ACLU Foundation of Massachusetts decided to replace its "parental leave" policy with a "family leave" policy that provides for as much as 12 weeks of leave not only for new parents, but also for employees who need to care for a spouse, child, or parent with a serious health condition.

According to Director Carol Rose, "We wanted a policy that took into account the fact that even employees who do not have children have family obligations." The policy was shaped by the belief that giving women "special treatment" can "backfire if the broader norms shaping the behavior of all employees do not change." When I was the dean of the Wilson School, I managed with the mantra "Family comes first"—any family—and found that my employees were both productive and intensely loyal.

None of these changes will happen by themselves, and reasons to avoid them will seldom be hard to find. But obstacles and inertia are usually surmountable if leaders are open to changing their assumptions about the workplace.

The use of technology in many high-level government jobs, for instance, is complicated by the need to have access to classified information. But in 2009, Deputy Secretary of State James Steinberg, who shares the parenting of his two young daughters equally with his wife, made getting such access at home an immediate priority so that he could leave the office at a reasonable hour and participate in important meetings via videoconferencing if necessary.

I wonder how many women in similar positions would be afraid to ask, lest they be seen as insufficiently committed to their jobs.

Revaluing Family Values

While employers shouldn't privilege parents over other workers, too often they end up doing the opposite, usually subtly, and usually in ways that make it harder for a primary caregiver to get ahead. Many people in positions of power seem to place a low value on child care in comparison with other outside activities.

"Of course I put my kids first! Look at how much I pay the nanny!!"

Consider the following proposition: An employer has two equally talented and productive employees. One trains for and runs marathons when he is not working. The other takes care of two children. What assumptions is the employer likely to make about the marathon runner? That he gets up in the dark every day and logs an hour or two running before even coming into the office, or drives himself to get out there even after a long day. That he is ferociously disciplined and willing to push himself through distraction, exhaustion, and days when nothing seems to go right in the service of a goal far in the distance. That he must manage his time exceptionally well to squeeze all of that in.

Be honest: Do you think the employer makes those same assumptions about the parent? Even though she likely rises in the dark hours before she needs to be at work, organizes her children's day, makes breakfast, packs lunch, gets them off to school, figures out shopping and other errands even if she is lucky enough to have a housekeeper—and does much the same work at the end of the day.

Cheryl Mills, Hillary Clinton's indefatigable chief of staff, has twins in elementary school; even with a fully engaged husband, she famously gets up at four every morning to check and send e-mails before her kids wake up.

Louise Richardson, now the vice chancellor of the University of St. Andrews, in Scotland, combined an assistant professorship in government at Harvard with mothering three young children. *She organized her time so ruthlessly that she always keyed in 1:11 or 2:22 or 3:33 on the microwave rather than 1:00, 2:00, or 3:00, because hitting the same number three times took less time.*

Elizabeth Warren, who is now running for the U.S. Senate in Massachusetts, has a similar story. When she had two young children and a part-time law practice, she struggled to find enough time to write the papers and articles that would help get her an academic position. In her words:

> I needed a plan. I figured out that writing time was when Alex was asleep. So the minute I put him down for a nap or he fell asleep in the baby swing, I went to my desk and started working on something—footnotes, reading, outlining, writing ... I learned to do everything else with a baby on my hip.

The discipline, organization, and sheer endurance it takes to succeed at top levels with young children at home is easily comparable to running 20 to 40 miles a week. But that's rarely how employers see things, not only when making allowances, but when making promotions. Perhaps because people choose to have children? People also choose to run marathons.

One final example: I have worked with many Orthodox Jewish men who observed the Sabbath from sundown on Friday until sundown on Saturday.

Jack Lew, the two-time director of the Office of Management and Budget, former deputy secretary of state for management and resources, and now White House chief of staff, is a case in point.

Jack's wife lived in New York when he worked in the State Department, so he would leave the office early enough on Friday afternoon to take the shuttle to New York and a taxi to his apartment before sundown. He would not work on Friday after sundown or all day Saturday. Everyone who knew him, including me, admired his commitment to his faith and his ability to carve out the time for it, even with an enormously demanding job.

It is hard to imagine, however, that we would have the same response if a mother told us she was blocking out mid-Friday afternoon through the end of the day on Saturday, every week, to spend time with her children. I suspect this would be seen as unprofessional, an imposition of unnecessary costs on co-workers. In fact, of course, one of the great values of the Sabbath—whether Jewish or Christian—is precisely that it carves out a family oasis, with rituals and a mandatory setting-aside of work.

Our assumptions are just that: things we believe that are not necessarily so. Yet what we assume has an enormous impact on our perceptions and responses. Fortunately, changing our assumptions is up to us.

Redefining the Arc of a Successful Career

The American definition of a successful professional is someone who can climb the ladder the furthest in the shortest time, generally peaking between ages 45 and 55. It is a definition well suited to the mid-20th century, an era when people had kids in their 20s, stayed in one job, retired at 67, and were dead, on average, by age 71.

It makes far less sense today. Men and women in good health can easily work until they are 75. They can expect to have multiple jobs and even multiple careers throughout their working life. Couples marry later, have kids later, and can expect to live on two incomes. They may well retire earlier—the average retirement age has gone down from 67 to 63—but that is commonly "retirement" only in the sense of collecting retirement benefits. Many people go on to "encore" careers.

Assuming the priceless gifts of good health and good fortune, a professional woman can thus expect her working life to stretch some 50 years, from her early or mid-20s to her mid-70s. It is reasonable to assume that she will build her credentials and establish herself, at least in her first career, between 22 and 35; she will have children, if she wants them, sometime between 25 and 45; she'll want maximum flexibility and control over her time in the 10 years that her children are 8 to 18; and she should plan to take positions of maximum authority and demands on her time after her children are out of the house.

'Investment Intervals' - Putting Money In The 'Family Bank'

Women who have children in their late 20s can expect to immerse themselves completely in their careers in their late 40s, with plenty of time still to rise to the top in their late 50s and early 60s. Women who make partner, managing director, or senior vice president; get tenure; or establish a medical practice before having children in their late 30s should be coming back on line for the most demanding jobs at almost exactly the same age.

Along the way, women should think about the climb to leadership not in terms of a straight upward slope, but as irregular stair steps, with periodic plateaus (and even dips) when they turn down promotions to remain in a job that works for their family situation; when they leave high-powered jobs and spend a year or two at home on a reduced schedule; or when they step off a conventional professional track to take a consulting position or project-based work for a number of years. I think of these plateaus as "investment intervals."

My husband and I took a sabbatical in Shanghai, from August 2007 to May 2008, right in the thick of an election year when many of my friends were advising various candidates on foreign-policy issues. We thought of the move in part as "putting money in the family bank," taking advantage of the opportunity to spend a close year together in a foreign culture. But we were also investing in our children's ability to learn Mandarin and in our own knowledge of Asia.

Peaking in your late 50s and early 60s rather than your late 40s and early 50s makes particular sense for women, who live longer than men. And many of the stereotypes about older workers simply do not hold. A 2006 survey of human-resources professionals shows that only 23 percent think older workers are less flexible than younger workers; only 11 percent think older workers require more training than younger workers; and only 7 percent think older workers have less drive than younger workers.

Straight Climb vs Planned Descent

Whether women will really have the confidence to stair-step their careers, however, will again depend in part on perceptions. Slowing down the rate of promotions, taking time out periodically, pursuing an alternative path during crucial parenting or parent-care years—all have to become more visible and more noticeably accepted as a pause rather than an opt-out. (In an encouraging sign, Mass Career Customization, a 2007 book by Cathleen Benko and Anne Weisberg arguing that "today's career is no longer a straight climb up the corporate ladder, but rather a combination of climbs, lateral moves, and planned descents," was a Wall Street Journal best seller.)

Institutions can also take concrete steps to promote this acceptance. For instance, in 1970, Princeton established a tenure-extension policy that allowed female assistant professors expecting a child to request a one-year extension on their tenure clocks. This policy was later extended to men, and broadened to include adoptions.

In the early 2000s, two reports on the status of female faculty discovered that only about 3 percent of assistant professors requested tenure extensions in a given year. And in response to a survey question, women were much more likely than men to think that a tenure extension would be detrimental to an assistant professor's career.

So in 2005, under President Shirley Tilghman, Princeton changed the default rule. The administration announced that all assistant professors, female and male, who had a new child would automatically receive a one-year extension on the tenure clock, with no opt-outs allowed. Instead, assistant professors could request early consideration for tenure if they wished. The number of assistant professors who receive a tenure extension has tripled since the change.

Family Over Presidency

One of the best ways to move social norms in this direction is to choose and celebrate different role models. New Jersey Governor Chris Christie and I are poles apart politically, but he went way up in my estimation when he announced that one reason he decided against running for president in 2012 was the impact his campaign would have had on his children.

He reportedly made clear at a fund-raiser in Louisiana that he didn't want to be away from his children for long periods of time; according to a Republican official at the event, he said that "his son [missed] him after being gone for the three days on the road, and that he needed to get back." He may not get my vote if and when he does run for president, but he definitely gets my admiration (providing he doesn't turn around and join the GOP ticket this fall).

If we are looking for high-profile female role models, we might begin with Michelle Obama. She started out with the same résumé as her husband, but has repeatedly made career decisions designed to let her do work she cared about and also be the kind of parent she wanted to be. She moved from a high-powered law firm first to Chicago city government and then to the University of Chicago shortly before her daughters were born, a move that let her work only 10 minutes away from home.

She has spoken publicly and often about her initial concerns that her husband's entry into politics would be bad for their family life, and about her determination to limit her participation in the presidential election campaign to have more time at home.

Even as first lady, she has been adamant that she be able to balance her official duties with family time. We should see her as a full-time career woman, but one who is taking a very visible investment interval. We should celebrate her not only as a wife, mother, and champion of healthy eating, but also as a woman who has had the courage and judgment to invest in her daughters when they need her most.

And we should expect a glittering career from her after she leaves the White House and her daughters leave for college.

Rediscovering the Pursuit of Happiness

One of the most complicated and surprising parts of my journey out of Washington was coming to grips with what I really wanted. I had opportunities to stay on, and I could have tried to work out an arrangement allowing me to spend more time at home. I might have been able to get my family to join me in Washington for a year; I might have been able to get classified technology installed at my house the way Jim Steinberg did; I might have been able to commute only four days a week instead of five. (While this last change would have still left me very little time at home, given the intensity of my job, it might have made the job doable for another year or two.)

But I realized that I didn't just need to go home. Deep down, I wanted to go home. I wanted to be able to spend time with my children in the last few years that they are likely to live at home, crucial years for their development into responsible, productive, happy, and caring adults. But also irreplaceable years for me to enjoy the simple pleasures of parenting—baseball games, piano recitals, waffle breakfasts, family trips, and goofy rituals. My older son is doing very well these days, but even when he gives us a hard time, as all teenagers do, being home to shape his choices and help him make good decisions is deeply satisfying.

Its Unfashionable To Mention Kids

The flip side of my realization is captured in Macko and Rubin's ruminations on the importance of bringing the different parts of their lives together as 30-year-old women:

If we didn't start to learn how to integrate our personal, social, and professional lives, we were about five years away from morphing into the angry woman on the other side of a mahogany desk who questions her staff's work ethic after standard 12-hour workdays, before heading home to eat moo shoo pork in her lonely apartment.

Women have contributed to the fetish of the one-dimensional life, albeit by necessity. The pioneer generation of feminists walled off their personal lives from their professional personas to ensure that they could never be discriminated against for a lack of commitment to their work. *When I was a law student in the 1980s, many women who were then climbing the legal hierarchy in New York firms told me that they never admitted to taking time out for a child's doctor appointment or school performance, but instead invented a much more neutral excuse.*

> *The conclusion is that women are delicate and weak. They should be given protection. They should not be ill-treated. Just like a father gives protection to the children. It does not mean it is ill-treatment. There is no question of. But protection. Otherwise, abaleva, they can be victimized by any man, because man is more powerful.*
>
> *~ Srila Prabhupada (Srimad-Bhagavatam 1.15.20 -- Los Angeles, November 30, 1973)*

Today, however, women in power can and should change that environment, although change is not easy. When I became dean of the Woodrow Wilson School, in 2002, I decided that one of the advantages of being a woman in power was that I could help change the norms by deliberately talking about my children and my desire to have a balanced life.

Thus, I would end faculty meetings at 6 p.m. by saying that I had to go home for dinner; I would also make clear to all student organizations that I would not come to dinner with them, because I needed to be home from six to eight, but that I would often be willing to come back after eight for a meeting. I also once told the Dean's Advisory Committee that the associate dean would chair the next session so I could go to a parent-teacher conference.

After a few months of this, several female assistant professors showed up in my office quite agitated. "You have to stop talking about your kids," one said. "You are not showing the gravitas that people expect from a dean, which is particularly damaging precisely because you are the first woman dean of the school." I told them that I was doing it deliberately and continued my practice, but it is interesting that gravitas and parenthood don't seem to go together.

Ten years later, whenever I am introduced at a lecture or other speaking engagement, I insist that the person introducing me mention that I have two sons. It seems odd to me to list degrees, awards, positions, and interests and not include the dimension of my life that is most important to me—and takes an enormous amount of my time.

As Secretary Clinton once said in a television interview in Beijing when the interviewer asked her about Chelsea's upcoming wedding: "That's my real life."

But I notice that my male introducers are typically uncomfortable when I make the request. They frequently say things like "And she particularly wanted me to mention that she has two sons"—thereby drawing attention to the unusual nature of my request, when my entire purpose is to make family references routine and normal in professional life.

"I Wish I Didn't Work So Hard."

This does not mean that you should insist that your colleagues spend time cooing over pictures of your baby or listening to the prodigious accomplishments of your kindergartner. It does mean that if you are late coming in one week, because it is your turn to drive the kids to school, that you be honest about what you are doing.

Indeed, Sheryl Sandberg recently acknowledged not only that she leaves work at 5:30 to have dinner with her family, but also that for many years she did not dare make this admission, even though she would of course make up the work time later in the evening. Her willingness to speak out now is a strong step in the right direction.

Seeking out a more balanced life is not a women's issue; balance would be better for us all. Bronnie Ware, an Australian blogger who worked for years in palliative care and is the author of the 2011 book The Top Five Regrets of the Dying, writes that the regret she heard most often was "I wish I'd had the courage to live a life true to myself, not the life others expected of me." The second-most-common regret was "I wish I didn't work so hard." She writes: "This came from every male patient that I nursed. They missed their children's youth and their partner's companionship."

'Happiness Project' - Let Us Start At Home

Juliette Kayyem, who several years ago left the Department of Homeland Security soon after her husband, David Barron, left a high position in the Justice Department, says their joint decision to leave Washington and return to Boston sprang from their desire to work on the "happiness project," meaning quality time with their three children. (She borrowed the term from her friend Gretchen Rubin, who wrote a best-selling book and now runs a blog with that name.)

It's time to embrace a national happiness project. As a daughter of Charlottesville, Virginia, the home of Thomas Jefferson and the university he founded, I grew up with the Declaration of Independence in my blood. Last I checked, he did not declare American independence in the name of life, liberty, and professional success. Let us rediscover the pursuit of happiness, and let us start at home.

Innovation Nation

As I write this, I can hear the reaction of some readers to many of the proposals in this essay: It's all fine and well for a tenured professor to write about flexible working hours, investment intervals, and family-comes-first management. But what about the real world?

> *Araksyamanah striya urvi balan. According to Vedic culture, first protection -- to the cows, to the women, to the brahmanas, to the children, and to the old man. This is the first business of the government, to give protection. Practically, there is no criminal charge against them -- against a brahmana, against a woman, a child. Suppose a child steals something. Who is going to prosecute him? It is not taken very seriously. So they require protection. Protection means to some extent no freedom. If I want to protect the child, then I sometimes say, "Don't do this." That is one of the items of the protection.*
>
> *Now in this age, Kali, these things will be lacking. First thing is that no protection for woman. Woman requires protection by the father, by the husband and by the elderly children. But that is now finished. Practically no protection. They are, under the name of so-called freedom, loitering in the street. It is a very abominable condition of life. Now these things are very prominent in the Western countries especially. In India they are still dragging the Vedic culture. So woman are given protection. The father gives protection to the woman, child, and up to sixteen years, utmost. Then she must be married. The father's duty will be finished when the daughter is given to a suitable boy to take charge. That is marriage system. Marriage system is necessary for social equilibrium. And it is the duty of the father to get the daughter married to a suitable boy. And when she is married, then the father's duty is finished. Unless she is married, the father's duty is not finished. This is Vedic culture. It is called kanya-daya. Kanya means daughter, and daya means obligation.*
>
> *~ Srila Prabhupada (Srimad-Bhagavatam 1.16.21 -- Los Angeles, July 11, 1974)*

Most American women cannot demand these things, particularly in a bad economy, and their employers have little incentive to grant them voluntarily. Indeed, the most frequent reaction I get in putting forth these ideas is that when the choice is whether to hire a man who will work whenever and wherever needed, or a woman who needs more flexibility, choosing the man will add more value to the company.

In fact, while many of these issues are hard to quantify and measure precisely, the statistics seem to tell a different story.

A seminal study of 527 U.S. companies, published in the Academy of Management Journal in 2000, suggests that "organizations with more extensive work-family policies have higher perceived firm-level performance" among their industry peers.

These findings accorded with a 2003 study conducted by Michelle Arthur at the University of New Mexico. Examining 130 announcements of family-friendly policies in The Wall Street Journal, Arthur found that the announcements alone significantly improved share prices.

In 2011, a study on flexibility in the workplace by Ellen Galinsky, Kelly Sakai, and Tyler Wigton of the Families and Work Institute showed that increased flexibility correlates positively with job engagement, job satisfaction, employee retention, and employee health.

This is only a small sampling from a large and growing literature trying to pin down the relationship between family-friendly policies and economic performance. Other scholars have concluded that good family policies attract better talent, which in turn raises productivity, but that the policies themselves have no impact on productivity. Still others argue that results attributed to these policies are actually a function of good management overall.

What is evident, however, is that many firms that recruit and train well-educated professional women are aware that when a woman leaves because of bad work-family balance, they are losing the money and time they invested in her.

Even the legal industry, built around the billable hour, is taking notice. Deborah Epstein Henry, a former big-firm litigator, is now the president of Flex-Time Lawyers, a national consulting firm focused partly on strategies for the retention of female attorneys.

In her book Law and Reorder, published by the American Bar Association in 2010, she describes a legal profession "where the billable hour no longer works"; where attorneys, judges, recruiters, and academics all agree that this system of compensation has perverted the industry, leading to brutal work hours, massive inefficiency, and highly inflated costs.

" We need more time, Kevin .. my lawyer barely KNOWS your lawyer. "

The answer—already being deployed in different corners of the industry—is a combination of alternative fee structures, virtual firms, women-owned firms, and the outsourcing of discrete legal jobs to other jurisdictions. Women, and Generation X and Y lawyers more generally, are pushing for these changes on the supply side; clients determined to reduce legal fees and increase flexible service are pulling on the demand side. Slowly, change is happening.

At the core of all this is self-interest. Losing smart and motivated women not only diminishes a company's talent pool; it also reduces the return on its investment in training and mentoring. In trying to address these issues, some firms are finding out that women's ways of working may just be better ways of working, for employees and clients alike.

Experts on creativity and innovation emphasize the value of encouraging nonlinear thinking and cultivating randomness by taking long walks or looking at your environment from unusual angles.

Integrating Non-Work Lives With The Work

In their new book, A New Culture of Learning: Cultivating the Imagination for a World of Constant Change, the innovation gurus John Seely Brown and Douglas Thomas write, "We believe that connecting play and imagination may be the single most important step in unleashing the new culture of learning."

Space for play and imagination is exactly what emerges when rigid work schedules and hierarchies loosen up. Skeptics should consider the "California effect." California is the cradle of American innovation—in technology, entertainment, sports, food, and lifestyles. It is also a place where people take leisure as seriously as they take work; where companies like Google deliberately encourage play, with Ping-Pong tables, light sabers, and policies that require employees to spend one day a week working on whatever they wish.

Charles Baudelaire wrote: "Genius is nothing more nor less than childhood recovered at will." Google apparently has taken note.

The books I've read with my children, the silly movies I've watched, the games I've played, questions I've answered, and people I've met while parenting have broadened my world. Another axiom of the literature on innovation is that the more often people with different perspectives come together, the more likely creative ideas are to emerge. Giving workers the ability to integrate their non-work lives with their work—whether they spend that time mothering or marathoning—will open the door to a much wider range of influences and ideas.

Enlisting Men

Perhaps the most encouraging news of all for achieving the sorts of changes that I have proposed is that men are joining the cause. In commenting on a draft of this article, Martha Minow, the dean of the Harvard Law School, wrote me that one change she has observed during 30 years of teaching law at Harvard is that today many young men are asking questions about how they can manage a work-life balance. And more systematic research on Generation Y confirms that many more men than in the past are asking questions about how they are going to integrate active parenthood with their professional lives.

Abstract aspirations are easier than concrete trade-offs, of course. These young men have not yet faced the question of whether they are prepared to give up that more prestigious clerkship or fellowship, decline a promotion, or delay their professional goals to spend more time with their children and to support their partner's career.

Yet once work practices and work culture begin to evolve, those changes are likely to carry their own momentum. Kara Owen, the British foreign-service officer who worked a London job from Dublin, wrote me in an e-mail:

> I think the culture on flexible working started to change the minute the Board of Management (who were all men at the time) started to work flexibly—quite a few of them started working one day a week from home.

Men have, of course, become much more involved parents over the past couple of decades, and that, too, suggests broad support for big changes in the way we balance work and family.

It is noteworthy that both James Steinberg, deputy secretary of state, and William Lynn, deputy secretary of defense, stepped down two years into the Obama administration so that they could spend more time with their children (for real).

Going forward, women would do well to frame work-family balance in terms of the broader social and economic issues that affect both women and men. After all, we have a new generation of young men who have been raised by full-time working mothers. Let us presume, as I do with my sons, that they will understand "supporting their families" to mean more than earning money.

(Anne-Marie Slaughter is a professor of politics and international affairs at Princeton University, and the mother of two teenage boys. She served as the director of policy planning at the State Department from 2009 to 2011.)

Source
Anne-Marie Slaughterjun, The Atlantic, June 13, 2012
Phillip Toledano

Protection does not mean negligence, no. Protection means to give her all facilities. That is protection. Just like father gives protection to the child... That does not mean neglecting. Similarly, a woman should be protected. It is not that neglecting. They misunderstand. In the Western countries maybe there is misbehavior, but actually we have seen, still going on in India, the woman is... That is the ideal given by Lord Ramacandra, how woman is given protection by the husband. Sitadevi was kidnapped. Ramacandra is the Supreme Lord. He could have married many thousands of Sita, but as the dutiful husband, to rescue one wife He killed the whole family of Ravana. This is protection. He killed the whole family of him. So woman requires protection, and the husband is responsible to give protection, the father is responsible to give protection, and the elderly children, they are responsible to give protection.

~ Srila Prabhupada (Srimad-Bhagavatam 3.28.18 -- Nairobi, October 27, 1975)

17

The Lost Art of Full-Time Homemaking

My heart aches tonight.

What about the children? The children without their mothers at home during the day? The children without their anchor in this storm-tossed world, without their sun to guide and steady them?

What about the mothers? The mothers adrift at sea, lost? The mothers who feel trapped in the drudgery of a day-job, who just want to go home, to make their home a beautiful place for the ones they love?

What about the families? The families fraying at the edges, care-worn and over-busy? The families who want to have time for each other, but don't know how to escape the unceasing, frantic busyness that is today?

My heart aches for the children, the mothers, and the families. It doesn't have to be this way.

The Only One

When I was in college about five years ago, I took a Sociology class. One day during a lecture about women in the workplace, the professor asked how many women in the class planned to stay home when they had kids. Out of at least one hundred female students, I was the only one who raised my hand.

I remember glancing around, feeling surprise and then sadness. A few girls were looking at me. I held my hand a little higher and caught the professor's eye.

"Only one," she said, her expression solemn. I think even she was surprised.

Only one.

Where are those women today, I wonder? They were my classmates and peers. I wonder how many of them are mothers now.

My heart aches tonight.

Homemaking Matters

Homemaking matters. Let me say that again. Homemaking matters! It is an honor and a blessing. It's not a dusty relic of days gone by; it's a desperately needed calling today.

When did homemaking become something to be ashamed of? When did it become sub-par, a menial task relegated to the uneducated or lazy? Why do I (still!) feel a twinge of embarrassment when I say "I'm a homemaker," to someone who asks me where I work?

Our society today is crumbling at its foundation. Mothers barely know their children, families rarely spend quality time together. We know more about the lives of our Facebook friends than the lives of the faces across the dinner table (if we even eat at the table anymore)...

We must stop the madness! We must take a stand for our families. We must reclaim the passion and dignity of homemaking.

Our families are depending on us!

You Are Not Alone

The role of women in today's culture is controversial and a topic of heated debate. I know that some women truly must work outside the home, and some women truly want to work outside the home.

My own dear mother has worked outside the home for as long as I can remember. She worked hard, raising me and my two brothers by herself. I thank God for her. She has sacrificed much.

My wish is not to criticize women who work outside the home or cast judgement at all. I only wish to encourage the woman who is or longs to be a full-time homemaker.

If you want to fill your home with the gentle, irreplaceable touch that only a woman can; if you want to be available to your husband and children every day; if you long to prepare nourishing, homemade meals; if you crave the energy and presence of mind to manage your home well, to heal, and to listen…

If that is you, sweet mother, I want you to know that you are not alone.

Your desire is good, natural, and right. Never let anyone make you feel ashamed or guilty about wanting to "just" be a homemaker. I believe with all my heart that there is no greater or more fulfilling calling for a woman.

> *When I left my career as a full time RN to be a homemaker when my first baby was born, I endured tons of criticism from coworkers, friends, and some extended family… I have not regretted our decision…and for those that see homemaking as a way out of a "real job", I have never worked harder in my life than as a stay at home wife and mommy!!! And there is nothing more fulfilling outside of living for God than seeing your baby's first steps or hearing those first sweet words! It has been well worth the sacrifice and God has blessed abundantly!*
>
> *~ D'Ann, June 16, 2013*

"…that they admonish the young women to love their husbands, to love their children, to be discreet, chaste, homemakers, good, obedient to their own husbands, that the word of God may not be blasphemed." Titus 2:4-5, NKJV

Again, I'm not trying to throw stones or stir up anger. But I love being a homemaker, and it saddens me that so many women who would love being homemakers, too, are missing out on such joy in their lives because of….what? Fear? Pressure? Ignorance? Circumstance?

My heart aches tonight.

My Choice

I had a choice. After I graduated from college, I worked as an elementary music teacher for two years. When I was pregnant with my first son, my husband and I discussed long and hard whether or not I should stay home with our son full-time after he was born, or go back to work.

We were scared, sure. We didn't want to lose my income. Could we afford it? But as we talked and prayed about it, it became clear that the more important question was: Could we afford not to?

Ultimately we decided that our baby needed his mom (and his mom needed her baby!) more than we needed the money. It was the right choice, and I have not regretted it for a moment.

What Is Lost Can Be Found

It seems that the art of full-time homemaking is slipping farther away with each passing generation. But all is not lost. I believe that

> *Thank you! I'm so glad that I'm able to be a homemaker. It's what I've always wanted to do, and every time I see my son grin at me, or give me a kiss, or reach for me in a crowded room, I'm so happy with the decision I made to stay home. It's not easy, and there are certainly days I question this choice, but in the end, it is what I want to do. I am passionate about motherhood. :)*
>
> *~ Stephanie, August 11, 2014*

more and more women are rediscovering the beauty and necessity of homemaking. They are choosing to invest in their families first, and our world is a better place because of it.

So I say a silent prayer for the families, the mothers, and the children. The ache in my heart eases a little, and I smile to myself. What is lost can be found. The lost art of homemaking can be rediscovered- one mother, one child, one happy family at a time.

Source
Stephanie Elliott, June 14, 2013, The Hidden Home Maker

The woman is known as a man's better half, so if she looks after the comfort of the man, a man is working and he looks after her comfort, then both will be satisfied and their spiritual life will progress. Woman is meant for certain duties; man is meant for... Man is meant for hard working, and woman is meant for homely comfort, love. So both of them, if they are situated in their respective duties under proper training, then this combination of man and woman will help both of them to make progress in spiritual life.
~ *Srila Prabhupada (Philosophical discussions, Auguste Comte)*

They Wear Nappies, Drink Cola And Don't Know How To Open A Book.

One Teacher's Terrifying Insight Into 5-Year-Olds Failed By Their Parents

A UK Case Study

We are failing our young children 'on a grand scale' when it comes to achieving basic levels of social and emotional development, experts have warned. Sir Michael Marmot, director of the University College London Institute of Health Equity, said social inequality is leaving two in every five children unable to perform simple life skills by the age of five.

He said markers of early child development were closely linked with deprivation – with the UK ranking 'badly' compared with other nations. These indicators include being able to dress and undress independently.

They also measure children's ability to maintain concentration, the level of interest shown in classroom activities. Other areas children might be scored on include understanding the difference

> More than 40% of children fail to meet key development indicators such as being able to dress and undress independently.
> They also show inability to maintain concentration or understand the difference between right and wrong.

between right and wrong, ability to use language, recognising familiar words and developing an interest in books.

Here, one teacher (wishes to remain anonymous) describes a day in the life of an affluent primary school. What she says will shock you...

Glancing at the clock, I realise it's time for me to change Lily's nappy. Past experience tells me she will make a fuss, so I doubt it will be a smooth operation. Of course, most babies dislike having their nappies changed, but that's the problem: Lily isn't a baby, she is five years old.

What's more, I'm not her mother, I am her primary school teacher. And Lily isn't the only child in my class who still wears nappies

It's not as if I am a teacher in a sink school, either. I work in an affluent town in the South of England, yet every day at my school we are dealing with the fallout of what can, at best, be described as parental irresponsibility, at worst, downright negligence. I teach children aged four and five, and, of course, accidents do happen

Problems: A schoolboy tries to solve a problem. A teacher's report reveals children aged five are not potty trained - and are left with rotten teeth

when it comes to young children using the loo. But almost every day I have to clear up after a child who has soiled himself.

These children don't have a medical condition. What they have are parents who think children will learn to use the lavatory by themselves, or that it is a school's responsibility to teach them.

So the news last week that most teachers have witnessed an increase in the number of children soiling themselves came as no surprise to me.

A survey carried out by the Association of Teachers and Lecturers, along with the charity Education and Resources for Improving Childhood Continence, also found that teachers believe primary schoolchildren are less independent than they were a decade ago. That, too, strikes a chord with me.

There is a child in my class who has serious dental problems because of her consumption of fizzy, sugary drinks. That's bad in itself, but the most worrying thing is that, at age five, she isn't independent enough to drink from a cup. She drinks these fizzy drinks from a baby's bottle.

These parents seem to believe that giving their children fundamental life skills isn't their responsibility. They think that it's the job of teachers

Lucy doesn't bring the bottle into school, but she told me without a hint of self-consciousness that she still drinks 'fizzy' from her 'baby

> *Children begotten under the rules and regulations of the scriptures generally become as good as the father and mother, but children born illegitimately mainly become varna-sankara. The varna-sankara population is irresponsible to the family, community and even to themselves. Formerly the varna-sankara population was checked by the observation of the reformatory method called garbhadhana-samskara, a child-begetting religious ceremony. In this verse we find that although King Puranjana had begotten so many children, they were not varna-sankara. All of them were good, well-behaved children, and they had good qualities like their father and mother.*
> ~ Srila Prabhupada (Srimad Bhagavatam 4.27.7)

bottle'. And her terrible tooth decay is testament to that. Her front teeth are like little black pegs.

The poor child also has real problems with speech. She can't pronounce many of the sounds because one needs a full set of teeth to do so.

I rang her home umpteen times to ask her mother to make a dental appointment. Eventually, under tremendous pressure from the school and the welfare department, whom I alerted, she did — and I assume the matter is being dealt with.

I have been a primary school teacher for eight years, and over the past few years I've witnessed a shocking decline in children's basic skills.

A 'Big Impact' On Adulthood

Research has found that the proportion of youngsters achieving a good level of development at age five stands at 59 per cent in England, up slightly on the year before but still not good enough, Sir Michael Marmot said.

'Only 59% of children were ranked at age five as having a good level of child development. Only 59%,' he said.

Hard workers: While these children from a Welsh primary engage, Alex Evans reveals many parents don't see it as their responsibility to give their youngsters life skills

'You think to yourself, how can it possibly be the case that 41% of children across the country are thought not to have a good level of child development?

'Surely there must be something wrong with the figures, you think to yourself, that's what I thought. How can that possibly be right?

'The fact is it could be right. We do really, really badly on international comparisons, really badly.'

He said a chart on international comparisons of child wellbeing puts Finland in front and the UK lagging behind.

He said the UK is also 'bumping along' and ranking about 25th on maths and science.

'This is a really brainy country, why shouldn't we be number one?', he said.

Sir Michael said the best universities in the country are also the best in Europe, but there are huge inequalities.

'We've got these huge inequalities which means that we're failing our children on a grand scale and it matters to their health, it matters

> *To check the increase of demoniac population, the Vedic civilization enacted so many rules and regulations of social life, the most important of which is the garbhadhana process for begetting good children. In Bhagavad-gita Arjuna informed Krsna that if there is unwanted population (varna-sankara), the entire world will appear to be hell. People are very anxious for peace in the world, but there are so many unwanted children born without the benefit of the garbhadhana ceremony, just like the demons born from Diti. Diti was so lusty that she forced her husband to copulate at a time which was inauspicious, and therefore the demons were born to create disturbances. In having sex life to beget children, one should observe the process for begetting nice children; if each and every householder in every family observes the Vedic system, then there are nice children, not demons, and automatically there is peace in the world. If we do not follow regulations in life for social tranquillity, we cannot expect peace. Rather, we will have to undergo the stringent reactions of natural laws.*
> ~ *Srila Prabhupada (Srimad Bhagavatam 3.17.15)*

to their wellbeing and the productivity of the country, it matters to the sort of society we want. And it matters all the way through.'

He said poor development in early childhood had a 'big impact' on the numbers in the UK who end up not in education, employment or training.

The school makes it clear that we expect children to be able to use a lavatory, button their coats and eat with a knife and fork by the time they begin full-time education, but far too many of them just can't. They've never been taught how.

These parents seem to believe that giving their children fundamental life skills isn't their responsibility. They think that it's the job of teachers.

Some parents see no problem at all with sending their little ones to school incontinent and unable to grasp even the most basic concepts of learning, with no ability to sit still even for a couple of minutes and a propensity to thump other children.

Every summer, I visit the homes of the 30 children who will join my class in the new school year. In about two-thirds of those homes, I see all the latest gadgets on display, including plasma television sets, games consoles and state-of-the-art computer equipment. What I don't see are any toys or books.

I make these visits both to introduce myself and to allay any fears that the children or their parents may have about the big step of starting school.

Sadly, in many cases, I really needn't bother. The parents don't even show me the courtesy of turning off the television during my

> *dosair etaih kula-ghnanam*
> *varna-sankara-karakaih*
> *utsadyante jati-dharmah*
> *kula-dharmas ca sasvatah*
> By the evil deeds of those who destroy the family tradition and thus give rise to unwanted children, all kinds of community projects and family welfare activities are devastated.
> ~ Bhagavad-gita 1.42

visit. Asking what they hope for from school and what their worries are, I'm met with blank stares.

When youngsters have absolutely no concept of numbers, it's simply impossible for teachers to focus on teaching what's called the Early Years Foundation Curriculum, which sets out very basic attainment targets — for example, being able to count from one to ten.

It might seem hard to believe, but many parents barely speak to their children, far less bother to educate them. A colleague told me that children in her class of five-year-olds are unable to speak in proper sentences. 'Give pencil,' a child will say.

I put it down to parents dumping their children in front of the TV rather than interacting with them. I've even had to give up on activities such as painting because many of the children in my classroom can't hold a paintbrush.

When I sat down with this little boy and tried to read with him, he tried to pull it open from its spine. He had no idea how to hold a pencil, and when I asked him what letter the word 'red' started with, it became apparent that he wasn't even sure what the colour red looked like

They've never done it at home, and they have such short concentration spans that after the first hesitant stroke of brush on paper, they are off, running up and down the classroom.

We are trained to teach the four and five-year-olds through play, but the sad truth is that many of our children just don't know how to play. They have never been exposed to imaginary games or make-believe at home.

They have never had to concentrate on building a tower out of Lego, never set up a toy railway track and pushed trains around it.

Tommy, a five-year-old in my class, was a whizz on the computer. He could manipulate a mouse with ease and was adept at opening programmes, but he had no idea how to even open a book.

When I sat down with this little boy and tried to read with him, he tried to pull it open from its spine. He had no idea how to hold a pencil, and when I asked him what letter the word 'red' started with, it became apparent that he wasn't even sure what the colour red looked like. He didn't know his colours.

Sadly, Tommy isn't alone. Many of the little ones I teach have trouble grasping the most basic of concepts. I tried to do a project on the seasons, but most of the class couldn't name them. When

I love my job, and I love seeing children grow, learn and flourish. What is so distressing is witnessing the way so many parents have simply abdicated responsibility over the past decade

I mentioned that a daffodil was growing, several children looked puzzled and asked me what the word 'growing' meant.

Of course, many parents do a wonderful job and try hard to expose their children to books, toys and time outdoors — but some parents don't.

As for bedtime, many of the children I teach simply don't have one. Some of my pupils arrive at school so exhausted from playing on their computers until the early hours of the morning that I regularly have to put them down for a nap in the afternoon.

They fall asleep instantly and miss out on whatever activity the rest of the class is engaged in. *I think the school I work in is probably a microcosm of Britain as a whole.*

Some pupils' parents are stockbrokers and bankers who commute to work in the City of London, but our catchment area also includes a deprived council estate where mainly white working-class families live. Some of the children I teach are immigrants.

What happens in my classroom is in no way extraordinary. Speaking to colleagues in other schools, my experience is representative of classrooms across the country.

lalayet panca varsani
dasa varsani tadayet
prapte tu sodase varse
putram mitravad acaret
This is the moral instruction of Canakya Pandita. Up to five years, don't chastise, don't take any action. Let him be free. Whatever he likes, he can do. Then after fifth year, for ten years you must be very strict. Then five years and ten years, fifteen. And when he is sixteen years, treat him like a friend. At that time, no stricture, than he will break. Only friendly advice. This is necessary. And from fifth year to fifteenth year you should chastise the sons and disciples just like tiger.
~ Srila Prabhupada (Interview with Mr. Koshi, Asst. Editor of The Current Weekly) -- April 5, 1977, Bombay

It just seems to me that many mums and dads have no understanding of their own responsibilities. And, working in this school, I sometimes feel that my heart will break because these children are so defenceless against the incompetence of their parents.

I love the little ones in my class, and it makes me sad and angry that some of them come to school in the winter without socks on. And let me be clear here: this is not down to poverty. Parents are simply failing to attend to such details. Instead, I keep a few pairs in my handbag, together with clean underwear.

No child should have cold feet, and no child should sit in soiled underclothes, but their parents don't seem to agree with those basic requirements.

It is very difficult to work with children when their parents seem to work against you. Teachers who try to instill boundaries and a sense of right and wrong often end up castigated by enraged parents — and, sadly, the senior management can't always be relied upon to stand up for their staff.

There was one boy, Jamie, in my class, who was quite a handful and was constantly spitting at other children. He seemed to especially dislike another little boy, Darren, calling him horrible names, hitting him and spitting at him.

Taking Jamie's mum aside one afternoon when she came to pick him up, I asked if we could have a quiet word. 'Would you mind backing me

---

So far the engagements of the woman class is concerned they are accepted as the power of inspiration for the man. As such the women are more powerful than the man because a mighty Julius Ceaser is controlled by a Cleopatra. Such powerful woman is controlled by shyness. Therefore, shyness of woman may not be eradicated. Once this control-valve is loosened the powerful woman can create havoc in the society by means of adulteration. Adulteration of woman means production of unwanted children known as Varnasankara which makes the world into disturbing condition constantly so much so as to turn it into inhabitable place for the saner section
   ~ *Srila Prabhupada (Srimad Bhagavatam 1.9.27)*

up on what I've told Jamie, that he can't spit at other children?' I asked her, smiling.

Her response left me flabbergasted. 'You're picking on my son. How dare you tell me how to bring him up!' she fumed.

She then made a formal complaint against me to the headmaster, and to my amazement, he advised that I apologise.

I did so because it didn't seem worth the hassle or aggravation of refusing. I didn't want her son, difficult as he was, to think he wasn't welcome in my classroom.

> Srila Jiva Gosvami remarks in this connection that every child, if given an impression of the Lord from his very childhood, certainly becomes a great devotee of the Lord like Maharaja Pariksit. One may not be as fortunate as Maharaja Pariksit to have the opportunity to see the Lord in the womb of his mother, but even if he is not so fortunate, he can be made so if the parents of the child desire him to be so. There is a practical example in my personal life in this connection. My father was a pure devotee of the Lord, and when I was only four or five years old, my father gave me a couple of forms of Radha and Krsna. In a playful manner, I used to worship these Deities along with my sister, and I used to imitate the performances of a neighboring temple of Radha-Govinda. By constantly visiting this neighboring temple and copying the ceremonies in connection with my own Deities of play, I developed a natural affinity for the Lord. My father used to observe all the ceremonies befitting my position. Later on, these activities were suspended due to my association in the schools and colleges, and I became completely out of practice. But in my youthful days, when I met my spiritual master, Sri Srimad Bhaktisiddhanta Sarasvati Gosvami Maharaja, again I revived my old habit, and the same playful Deities became my worshipful Deities in proper regulation. This was followed up until I left the family connection, and I am pleased that my generous father gave the first impression which was developed later into regulative devotional service by His Divine Grace. Maharaja Prahlada also advised that such impressions of a godly relation must be impregnated from the beginning of childhood, otherwise one may miss the opportunity of the human form of life, which is very valuable although it is temporary like others.
>
> ~ Srila Prabhupada (Srimad Bhagavatam 1.12.30)

I love my job, and I love seeing children grow, learn and flourish. What is so distressing is witnessing the way so many parents have simply abdicated responsibility over the past decade.

Some mums and dads seem to think that their job is to give their children whatever they want, and the dreary stuff — manners, discipline and boundaries — should be left to teachers like me.

But the joy of childhood isn't about having free rein to do whatever they want as long as it doesn't inconvenience their parents.

Surely, the joy of childhood is about the incredible journeys of discovery that children make. Surely, the wonder of being a child lies in the abundance of learning — from the colours in the rainbow to how to eat like a grown-up.

Tragically, many of the youngsters in my classroom are experiencing a horribly stunted childhood. They are painfully aware of adult concepts like binge-drinking, yet can't recite a single nursery rhyme.

I shudder to think what the future holds for them.

Source
Alex Evans, The Daily Mail, 16th February 2012
Glenys Roberts, The Daily Mail, 15 February 2012
Jane Fields, 18 February 2012, The Daily Mail

19

Too Busy To Potty Train Your Child?

Meet The Experts Who Say They Can Get The Job Done In Just Two Days - For $1,750

A new trend in outsourced parenting is taking hold among busy mothers and fathers - professional potty-training services.

NYC Potty Training is just one of the companies that has emerged recently, with experts for hire who claim to be able to teach kids to use the toilet in just one or two days.

But the speedy lessons come at a steep price; a recommended two-day session costs a whopping $1,750, and one-day sessions will set you back $925.

For parents like Molly Goldberg, however, who hired NYC Potty Training founder Samantha Allen

Outsourced parenting: A new trend is taking hold among busy mothers and fathers - professional potty-training services, which can cost $1,750 for a two-day session

to train her three-year-old son Sam in time for summer camp, it's well worth the price tag.

The working mom from Roslyn, New York, told ABC News that she was 'frustrated' and had 'little patience' for Sam's aversion to going to the bathroom.

So when she spotted a post about NYC Potty Training on Facebook, she decided to give it a shot.

Ms Allen, an early childhood education specialist and former applied behavioral analysis teacher for children with special needs, came to her house loaded with toys and games to coax Sam to the bathroom.

Finally, after two-and-a-half hours of sitting and waiting with him, her method proved successful.

After that, Sam was much less apprehensive, with his mom taking him to the bathroom every 30 minutes to get him used to it. And just a few days later, he was fully potty-trained and has woken up dry every morning since the training session.

Potty expert: NYC Potty Training founder Samantha Allen is an early childhood education specialist who uses toys and games to coax kids into using the bathroom

Since its launch last month, NYC Potty Training has proved a huge hit among New York parents, but it's by no means the only company offering similar services.

Ashley Hickey, a self-described Potty Training Specialist and the owner of Successful Potty Training, hosts two-hour workshops for parents and teachers in Connecticut.

Bhagavan dasa: But actually, our women are so qualified in so many ways, but these girls who simply work in the city can do nothing. They can't cook, they can't clean, they can't sew.

Prabhupada: All rubbish, these modern girls, they are all rubbish. Therefore they are simply used for sex satisfaction. Topless, bottomless...

~ Srila Prabhupada (Morning Walk -- May 27, 1974, Rome)

She also provides 'intensive potty training' sessions for $75 per hour, with a focus on children with special needs.

Individual consultations, which take an hour and are typically done over the phone, cost $200.

And 'Potty Whisperer' Adriana Vermillion hosts five-day 'boot camp sessions' across the country aimed at getting kids potty-trained.

It may seem like an unlikely service to shell out on, but Ms Goldberg explains that for some parents, it's a necessity.

What's more, 'people spend money on all sorts of things,' she said. 'Going out, personal trainers.'

Source:
Margot Peppers, The Daily Mail
9 July 2014
Genevieve Shaw Brown Via Good Morning America, Jul 8, 2014, ABC News.

20

Married Couples' Health Suffers

When Men Earn Less Than Wives

Men whose wives earn more income are more likely to use erectile dysfunction medication than those who outearn their wives, even when the inequality is small, according to a new study.

Researchers looking at more than 2,00,000 married couples in Denmark from 1997 to 2006 also found that wives who outearned their husbands were more likely to suffer from insomnia and to use anti-anxiety medication.

They did not find these effects for unmarried couples or for men earning less than their wives prior to marriage.

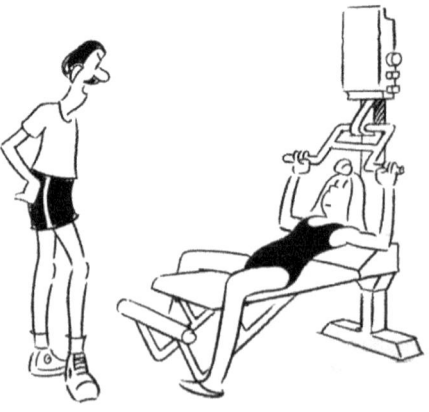

"I don't mind you earning more money than I do, or driving a more expensive car, but do you have to bench-press more than I do, too?"

The finding appeared online in Personality and Social Psychology Bulletin.

Career Woman - The Violence of Modern Jobs And The Lost Art of Home Making

Source
ANI : Washington, Sat Feb 09, 2013
Indian Express, Feb 09, 2013

21

Women Should Do All the Housework To Avoid Divorce

Study Suggests

A recent Norwegian study found that the divorce rates for couples who share housework are fifty percent higher than for couples in which the wife assumes the sole responsibility for household chores — and implicitly suggests that couples who share housework value marriage less, or that women nagging their partners about helping out around the house may lead to divorce. So much for equality between the sexes.

"The more a man does in the home, the higher the divorce rate," said Thomas Hansen, co-author of the study (news.com). The researchers did not find a cause-and-effect relationship between the man's duties at home, but rather chalk the higher divorce rate up to modern attitudes. "Modern couples are just that, both in the way they divide up the chores and in their perception of marriage."

Maybe couples who share housework just don't find marriage to be as sacred as more "traditional" couples do. So if you share housework, you aren't as committed to your marriage?

A Step Backwards

The way this study has been presented is a huge step back in the quest for gender equality. Hansen seems to suggest that it is

beneficial for women to do the majority of housework, to avoid nagging their partners and causing stress in the relationship. "There could be less quarrels," he said, "since you can easily get into squabbles if both have the same roles and one has the feeling that the other is not pulling his or her own weight."

Maybe so, but Hansen seems to suggest that women should just bear down and take care of all the housework. Why not encourage men to take over the household duties?

> Woman should be expert in cooking. That is their natural tendency. They should be educated how to cook nicely, how to please the husband, how to take care of the children. This is Vedic civilization. In the beginning a woman, childhood, she's trained up by the mother. Then as soon as she is married, she's transferred to the care of mother-in-law. There she is trained up. Then she becomes very good housewife, takes care of household affairs, husband, children, and home becomes happy. What is this nonsense, divorce? There is no such thing in the Vedic civilization, divorce. You must accept whatever God has given you as husband or wife, you must. They had no thinking even, idea of divorce. One may not agree with the husband. That is natural. Sometimes we do not agree. But there is no question of divorce.
> ~ Srila Prabhupada (Room Conversation, July 7, 1976, Baltimore)

In June 2012, the Bureau of Labor Statistics found that all women (even those with full time jobs) spend more time on household duties than men, about 2.6 hours per day compared to 2.1 hours. Women still do the vast majority of daily cooking and cleaning, as well as childcare, while men spend more time on yard work and home maintenance projects.

Who does what in your home? Is strict division of labor the answer to a happy marriage? Or is cooperation and the sharing of duties the best way to be fulfilled in a relationship?

Source
Anna Klenke, October 3, 2012, Care2
Maureen Shaw, October 6, 2012
Cindy Stauffer, Sep 12, 2013, Lancaster Online

Wives Really Are The Glue

That Hold Marriages Together

Those Who Calm Down Quickly After Arguments Have The Best Relationships

If you're the type of woman who calms down quickly after a row, congratulations.

Your relationship is on solid ground – no matter how long your other half sulks for.

According to research, the happiest marriages are those where the wife cools off quickly after a fight, even if her husband stays angry. The secret to wedded bliss? When it comes to keeping the

peace, it is more important for wives to calm down after a heated argument than husbands.

Scientists said that women are better at starting those difficult conversations that will solve the problem and allow both parties to move on – but only if they have regained their composure first.

And ironically, they found that if the husband attempts to start those conversations himself, his spouse will criticise him for trying to resolve things too quickly.

'Argument over. How about a nice cup of tea?'

Lead author Lian Bloch, an assistant psychology professor at Berkeley and Stanford universities in the US, said: 'When it comes to managing negative emotion during conflict, wives really matter. Emotions such as anger and contempt can seem very threatening for couples.

'But our study suggests that if spouses, especially wives, are able to calm themselves, their marriages can continue to thrive.'

The Canakya Pandita says,
aja-yuddhe muni-sraddhe prabhate megha-dumbare
dampatih kalahe caiva bambharambhe laghu-kriya
The funeral ceremony of a sage who died in the forest, a fight between two goats, a thunder clap in the morning, a quarrel between husband and wife–all begin in grand style but the outcome is insignificant.

In India, there is no question of divorce. So nobody takes very serious care when there is fight between husband and wife. Even they say: "I'm going to immediately leave you, going to kill you..." and so many things. But after an hour, everything is finished. No more quarrel.
~ Srila Prabhupada (Srimad-Bhagavatam 5.5.3 -- Stockholm, September 9, 1973)

The researchers studied more than 80 middle-aged and older couples by videotaping them and analysing how they interacted, taking into account factors including body language, facial expressions, tone of voice and conversation topics.

According to Berkeley College, 'time and again they found that marriages in which wives quickly calmed down during disputes were ultimately shown to be the happiest, both in the short and long run'.

In contrast, the husband's emotional regulation had 'little or no bearing on long-term marital satisfaction'.

The happiest marriages were those in which women used what the researchers called 'constructive communication' to temper disagreements.

Berkeley College psychologist Robert Levenson, a senior author of the study, said: 'When wives discuss problems and suggest solutions, it helps couples deal with conflicts.

> *In Vedic society no girl was allowed to remain independent and unmarried. Independence for women means they become like prostitutes, struggling to capture some man who will take care of her. In this way the so-called independent woman has to work very hard to make herself attractive by artificially wearing cosmetics, mini-skirts and so many other things. Formerly the girl would be married to a suitable boy at a very early age. But although a girl was married early she did not stay with her husband immediately, but was gradually trained in so many ways how to cook, clean and serve her husband in so many ways -- up until the time of puberty. So all the time there was no anxiety because a girl would know -- I have got a husband, and the boy would know I have got this girl as my wife. Therefore when the boy and girl would come of age there was no chance of illicit sex-life. And the psychology is the first boy that a girl accepts in marriage, that girl will completely give her heart to, and this attachment on the girl's side for her husband becomes more and more strong. So you are fortunate. Go on in this present attitude, serve your husband always and in this way your life will be perfect, and together husband and wife go back home -- back to Godhead."*
>
> *~ Srila Prabhupada (Letter to Naiskarmi devi dasi, 28th July, 1973)*

'This may not work so well for husbands, whom wives often criticise for leaping into problem-solving mode too quickly.'

The research was part of the long-term monitoring of 156 heterosexual couples in California. Every five years since 1989 they have updated researchers on how happy their marriages are.

Source
By Daniel Bates, New York, The Daily Mail, 5 November 2013
John Gottman, Nan Silver, March 01, 1994, Psychology Today

23

Adopting The Fifties Lifestyle

To Save Their Marriages

Woman, 49, who lives like it's 1950, claims cooking, cleaning and sewing makes her a better wife

A wife who went back in time to live like it's still the 1950s claims that the retro lifestyle has saved her marriage.

Mandy Jones, 49, spends her free time cooking, cleaning and darning her husband Gary's socks.

She also dresses in vintage frocks, drives a 1949 Chevrolet and listens to rockabilly records on her jukebox, just like teens from sixty years ago.

Mandy, from Tamworth, Staffordshire, claims going back in time has saved her marriage which was 'stuck in a rut'.

Controversially, the part-time caterer, said that all women should adopt the lifestyle if they want to keep their man happy.

She said: 'It may seem strange and we get the odd nasty comment, but this way of life works for us and has saved our marriage.

Even the telephone they use is a 50s model

'We love everything about the 1950s, from the clothes to the way of life. Since we started living like this I've been a better wife and Gary and I are closer than ever.

'We should all take advice from our grandparents and start living the Fifties way.'

After deciding something needed to be done to keep her marriage to Gary, 48, alive, she travelled back in time to the 1950s.

Now every night when Gary comes home from work, his dutiful wife has dinner on the table - and they tuck into wholesome 1950s food in their American diner-style kitchen.

The couple now also spend their free time Lindy Hop dancing or exploring local vintage fairs.

When they first met 30 years ago they bonded over their love of rockabilly and Fifties fashion. But five years ago their passion for the decade reached new heights when they decided to go back in time and live like it is the 1950s.

Bored of their everyday life, Mandy said she was willing to go to extreme lengths to save their marriage, saying: 'Gary and I were sick of the same routine and we were bickering on a daily basis.

'We spent our weekends drinking at the pub until the early hours and it just got so boring.'

Vintage memorabilia: The home of Mandy and Gary Jones, from Tamworth in Staffordshire who live as though it was still the 1950s, is filled with fifties memorabilia

The couple decided to take the plunge and dedicate every aspect of their lives to the decade, decorating their entire house - and even building a 1950s-style diner.

Mandy perfected vintage hairstyles and started making her own retro-style clothes in a bid to impress her husband.

Now, instead of booze-filled weekends, the pair go dancing together and take trips in their Chevrolet to vintage fairs.

She said: 'We're a lot happier living in the 1950s way, it has improved our marriage and enriched our lives.

'Before, we didn't have much to excite us apart from drinking but now we do all sorts together and it keeps our relationship fresh.'

Mandy says that all couples should embrace her lifestyle because the divorce rates were lower in the 50s.

'After a bad day there is nothing better than putting our jukebox on and doing a quick Lindy Hop.'

Mandy is now encouraging others to follow in her and Gary's footsteps, claiming they too could save their marriage.

She said: '1950s marriages definitely work better than marriages these days.

Just like sometimes in the Vedic conception the wife is considered as dharma-patni, religious wife. Means wife helps the husband in the matter of his religious life. That is found in, still in Hindu family: the man is worshiping the Deity and the woman is helping about the paraphernalia Deity worship, helping the husband so that he can immediately come into the Deity room and begin worshiping comfortably. So woman should always be engaged to assist the man in every respect in his religious life, in his social life, in his family life. That is real benefit of conjugal life. But if the woman does not agree with the man, and the man treats the woman as his servant, that is not good. The man should give the woman all protection and the woman should give all service to the man. That is ideal life, family life, conceived in the Vedic way of life.

~ Srila Prabhupada (Philosophical discussions, Auguste Comte)

'The divorce rate is so high at the moment and it never used to be in the past. We should all take advice from our grandparents and start living the Fifties way.'

The divorce rate in 1950 was 26 per cent and 42 per cent in 2013.

Source:
Bianca London, The Daily Mail, 23 July 2014

We shall teach the girls two things. One thing is how to become chaste and faithful to their husband and how to cook nicely... These two qualifications required. She must learn how to prepare first-class foodstuff, and she must learn how to become chaste and faithful to the husband. Only these two qualification required. Then her life is successful. Educate the girls how to become faithful, chaste wife and how to cook nicely. Let them learn varieties of cooking. Is very difficult? And by fifteenth, sixteenth year they should be married. And if they are qualified, it will be not difficult to find out a nice husband. Here the boys, they do not want to marry because they are not very much inclined to marry unchaste wife. They know it, that "I shall marry a girl, she is unchaste." What do you think?

~ Srila Prabhupada (Morning Walk, July 10, 1975, Chicago, USA)

24

Happy Wife Makes Happy Marriages

A husband who is unhappy with his marriage is still likely to be happy with his life – if his wife gives their marriage high marks, a new study suggests. 'Older husbands and wives in better marriages are more satisfied with their lives,' says Vicki Freedman, a research professor at the University of Michigan Institute for Social Research.

'But overall life satisfaction for an unhappily married man depends on how his wife describes their relationship. If she describes their marriage as higher quality, his life satisfaction is buoyed – even if he gives the marriage a less glowing assessment,' sayd Freedman,

a co-author with Rutgers University sociologist Deborah Carr. The research is among the first to examine the influence of his and

> Hayagriva: *The role of woman he envisioned as that of man's companion. He says, "The first aspect, then, under which positivism considers women is simply as the companion of man, irrespective of her maternal duties," and that this friendship or companionship has as its basis sex. He says, "Conjugal union becomes a perfect ideal of friendship, yet still more beautiful than friendship, because each possesses and is possessed by the other. For perfect friendship, difference of sex is essential as excluding the possibility of rivalry." So he felt that sex, there can actually be very little friendship between men, because there's no sexual basis, that sex is the basis for the friendship between the sexes.*
>
> Prabhupada: Hmm. So there is sex, sexual necessity and the bodily demand. So woman not only give the sex pleasure to the man, but woman should prepare good foodstuff also for the man. The man is working very hard. When he comes home, if the wife supplies him good foodstuff and nice comfort, then the home becomes very happy. That is practical experience. So after hard working, when man comes home, if he finds out good foodstuff and nicely satisfied by eating, and then the woman gives satisfaction by sex, then both of them remain fully satisfied, and then they can improve their real business, spiritual understanding, because human life is meant for making progress in spiritual understanding. Spiritual, first of all they must know that the spirit soul is the basis of material life even, and the body is built up on the soul, and within the body there is soul. This understanding is required both for the man and the woman. This we see in the instruction of Kapiladeva. Kapiladeva is the son of Devahuti, and He is engaged in teaching the mother. So a woman, either as daughter, as wife or mother, remains subordinate and gets knowledge from the man, either from the father or the husband or son. Then that life is elevated. We find also in the conjugal life of Lord Siva and Parvati, in the Puranas we see always Parvati is questioning and Lord Siva is answering. In this way woman is elevated, and the comforts given by the woman, comforts of the tongue, of the belly, and the genital, in this way, cooperative life, both of them becomes advanced in spiritual life. (Philosophical discussions, Auguste Comte)

her marriage appraisals on psychological well-being among older couples.

'Marital quality is an important buffer against the health-depleting effects of later-life stressors such as care-giving, and a critical resource as couples manage difficult decisions regarding their care in later life,' Carr says.

Freedman and Carr analysed 2009 data from a sample of 394 couples who were part of the ISR Panel Study of Income Dynamics, a national panel study of a representative sample of US families. At least one spouse in each couple was aged 60 or older.

They found that life satisfaction and momentary happiness did not differ significantly by gender.

Both husbands and wives, on average, rated their general life satisfaction as 5 out of 6 and happiness very close to 5.

They also found that husbands rated their marriages slightly more positively than wives, on average. 'For both husbands and wives, being in a better-rated marriage was linked to greater life satisfaction and happiness,' Carr says.

'But wives' assessments of the marriage are more important in some respects than their husbands' reports,' she says.

The study was published in the Journal of Marriage and Family.

Source
Editorial Team, The Hindu, September 13, 2014
With inputs from PTI
News Nation, September 13, 2014
Editorial Team, The Health Site, Sep 14, 2014

25

The Power of Less

The Fine Art of Limiting Yourself to the Essential....In Business And In Life

By Leo Babauta

What? You are advising us to learn to slow down things in life? With so much competition in every walk of life? Yes! And I don't want you to get it wrong. When everyone in every conceivable medium is exhorting you with catchy slogans like act fast, hurry, do not lose time thinking, move swiftly, how sane is my advise to learn to slow things down, you might wonder. Believe me (and start putting this into practice from the moment you finish reading this article), you will get the best out of life only when you can slow things down.

How Does Slowing Down Help Me?

1. Slowing down ensures you do not under perform because you acted in haste & hurry.

2. It gives you enough time to space out your thoughts and sharpens your decision making ability.

3. You avoid loss of time and valuable resources which may occur due to repetition or re-working needed because of below par product, service or outcome.

4. The process of experiencing doing a certain act or ritual is as satisfying and important as the outcome itself. There is a feel-good factor resulting from these.

5. You will reduce adverse emotional impacts and ensure stress free health & wellness when you give it the required time.
6. It will give you a sense of fulfillment.

What Are Things That Slowing Down Should Apply to?

Slowing down is as important in personal, home situations as much as it is for professional work. It applies to such basic chores as eating food, driving your car, doing very mundane things at home as does it to managing your work-at the counter, at the back office, in a plant or for that matter, in any vocation.

Why Do We Do Things in Hurry & How to Practice Slowing Down?

We do things in a hurry because we are not focused on the task at hand. We tend not to be with the job we are currently engaged in, because of stress we create ourselves with trying achieve too many things in too little time. Stress is also caused by external circumstances like pressure from demands at work, fast paced life, family & finance issues etc.

We tend to get distracted, one reason for which is lack of focusing within.

Is Slowing Down a Realistic Option? Does It Always Help?

Slowing down is not procrastinating. Slowing down is also not putting things off out of laziness or indifference. It just means that you give every act the time it needs to do it fully, proficiently and making sure you live that experience.

Living that experience is key to derive full benefit both physically and emotionally. In a foundation course on living we attended, the instructor handed every one of us a single grape fruit each and told us to just hold in hand for a while, until every one received a piece each. We would, in any other situation, popped it quickly in our mouths and before we had even known, chewed and swallowed it as if it was a non event. We waited for her next instructions. She asked us to place it in our mouth without biting into it. We were then asked to roll it into the mouth a few times and feel its presence, aroma and texture. We then had to bite it slowly and savor the juice slowly, without rushing to suck it all down. We were then to experience its lasting taste lingering in our mouth for some time.

I can cite another very relevant example. I have been building a niche website, an online business of my own with the help of a highly popular and efficient system that teaches us, not just with a suite of tools but with a sustained counseling to do it slow, like the tortoise. In fact, the tortoise is their mascot, to emphasize the cardinal approach to success. Most people (me included, initially) are only to eager and impulsive to rush but they remind us all the time to be the tortoise!

The difference between doing things routinely, mechanically and without conscious experience and the one we experienced as I narrated above is quite discernible.

Always remember to step back and take time to experience when you do anything. Give it the space and time it needs to accomplish it in a way that you cherish doing it. This will also help you in building your health & happiness.

These sayings, about the conscious slow approach, though some of them old, are still as relevant today. Here are those:

1. Slow and steady wins the race
2. Do not marry in haste, to repent at leisure
3. Slow down and experience life. It's not only the scenery you miss by going to fast – you also miss the sense of where you are going and why.

> *I hate it. All these consultants are pretending to be happy and they are taking happiness pills. I get to sleep only 3–4 hours a day. Remember the fancy five-star hotel? I am working almost 20 hours a day and I don't even enjoy it. Fancy breakfast? We never have time to have that. Fancy lunch, dinner? It's just a sandwich in front of our Excel spreadsheets.*
>
> *Oh, by the way, instead of enjoying a champagne, I stare at spreadsheets during my entire business class flights, too. The fancy salary? I never have time to spend a single penny of it.*
>
> ~ *Ali Mese*

4. It gets to the point where you're hot, you're hot, and when you're not, you're not. It's so true. I have to slow down soon. There is no other option as we are overwhelmed by the increasing demands in our lives.

Reference
How to Slow Down Time With Your Mind, By Leo Babauta

Practicing sense control. Just like a diseased person. By controlling according to the prescription of the doctor, he reduces his suffering. The fever diminishes from 105 degrees to 102, then 100, then 99, then 98 -- he is cured. Similarly, we have to reduce the temperature. We haven't got to increase the temperature. We are thinking that by increasing the temperature we shall be happy. We do not know that by increasing the temperature we shall never be happy. We have to decrease the temperature. There is a very nice story. Perhaps I have many times told you, that there was a householder, a very rich man. His wife was sick and the maidservant was also sick. So the gentleman called for a doctor, and the doctor treated both the patients, and the doctor said that "Your wife has got 98 temperature, nothing serious. But your maidservant, she has got 104 temperature, so she should be taken care of." Now, the housewife, she became angry. She told the doctor, "Oh, I am the head of the family. I have got only 98 temperature? And my maidservant has got 104? So you are not a doctor!" So that is going on. From 104 we want to increase. But when the temperature reaches 107 degrees, death will come. So the modern civilization is increasing the temperature. We have come to the point of 107 degree-atom bomb. So we are prepared to kill ourselves. This increasing of temperature of material enjoyment will never make us happy. We have to decrease the temperature. We have to come to the point of 97, not to 107.

~ Srila Prabhupada (Lecture, Bhagavad-gita 5.22-29 -- New York, August 31, 1966)

26
Slow Movements

The Slow Movement advocates a cultural shift toward slowing down life's pace. It began with Carlo Petrini's protest against the opening of a McDonald's restaurant in Piazza di Spagna, Rome in 1986 that sparked the creation of the Slow Food organization. Over time, this developed into a subculture in other areas, such as Slow Cities, Slow living, Slow Travel, and Slow Design.

Geir Berthelsen and his creation of The World Institute of Slowness presented a vision in 1999 for an entire 'Slow Planet' and a need to teach the world the way of Slow. Carl Honoré's 2004 book, In Praise of Slowness, first explored how the Slow philosophy might be applied in every field of human endeavour and coined the phrase "Slow Movement." The Financial Times said the book is "to the Slow Movement what Das Kapital is to communism."

Honoré describes the Slow Movement thus:

"It is a cultural revolution against the notion that faster is always better. The Slow philosophy is not about doing everything at a snail's pace. It's about seeking to do everything at the right speed. Savoring the hours and minutes rather than just counting them. Doing everything as well as possible, instead of as fast as possible. It's about quality over quantity in everything from work to food to parenting."

Professor Guttorm Fløistad summarizes the philosophy, stating:

"The only thing for certain is that everything changes. The rate of change increases. If you want to hang on you better speed up. That is the message of today. It could however be useful to remind everyone that our basic needs never change. The need to be seen and appreciated! It is the need to belong. The need for nearness and care, and for a little love! This is given only through slowness in human relations. In order to master changes, we have to recover slowness, reflection and togetherness. There we will find real renewal."

The Slow Movement is not organized and controlled by a single organization. A fundamental characteristic of the Slow Movement is that it is propounded, and its momentum maintained, by individuals who constitute the expanding global community of Slow. Its popularity has grown considerably since the rise of Slow Food and Slow City in Europe, with Slow initiatives spreading as far as Australia and Japan.

Cittaslow (Slow City)

Cittaslow movement is to resist the homogenization and globalization of towns and cities. It seeks to improve the quality and enjoyment of living by encouraging happiness and self-determination.

Everything is going on. Your motorcar is going on. You are going on. We have a big city, especially in Europe, America, simply going on. This way, this... Whoosh, whoosh, whoosh. No rest. This is called jagat. Where he is going on? You have heard Rabindranath Tagore, poet Tagore. He wrote one article that "When I was in London I saw the people are walking very fast, the cars are going very fast. But I was thinking that 'This England is a small island; they may not fall down in the sea.'" (laughter) If you let loose your dog, it will go on this way, this way, this way, this way, this way. (laughter) This is jagat, going on. Going on, but condition: "You cannot go beyond this."
~ Srila Prabhupada (Lecture, Srimad-Bhagavatam 1.1.2 -- London, August 16, 1971)

Slow Art

Slow Art is an emerging movement evolving out of a philosophy of art and life expounded by the artist Tim Slowinski. It advocates appreciating an art work in itself as opposed to a rapid, flitting witnessing of art common in a hectic societal setting.

Another interpretation of Slow Art relates to creating art in a slow way. This practice is about being mindful of detail, valuing the history inherent in re-usable materials, putting time into creating small items. The practice encourages the maker to be naturally  meditative as they create. "Slow" ends up being a way of being.

Slow Church

Slow Church is a movement in Christian praxis which integrates Slow Movement principles into the structure and character of the local church. The phrase was introduced in 2008 by Christian bloggers working independently who imagined what such a "Slow Church" might look like. Over the next several years, the concept continued to be discussed online and in print by various writers and ministers.

In July 2012, a three-day conference titled Slow Church: Abiding Together in the Patient Work of God was held on the campus of DePaul University in Chicago on the topic of Slow Church.

Ethics, ecology, and economy are cited as areas of central concern to Slow Church. Slow Church is described as a "conversation" not a movement and has New Monasticism as an influence.

It has emphases on non-traditional ways for churches to operate and on "conversation" over dogma and hierarchy,

Slow Education

Slow education is based upon Socratic, adaptive and non-standards based approaches to teaching. Slow education is in part a reaction to the overly compacted course content requirements teachers are experiencing from nationalized curricula worldwide, which many educators find students cannot cover in a single year with sufficient depth. Slow education is also a reaction to the proliferation of standardized testing, favoring instead qualitative measures of student and teacher success.

Slow education is frequently a feature in free, democratic and home schools. However, it can be a significant element in any classroom, including those in college preparatory and rigorous environments. The term "slow education" was derived from the distinction between slow food and fast food or junk food, and is an effort to associate quality, culture and personalization with quality schooling.

Slow Fashion

The term "Slow Fashion" was coined by Kate Fletcher in 2007 (Centre for Sustainable Fashion, UK). "Slow fashion is not a seasonal trend that comes and goes, but a sustainable fashion movement that is gaining momentum."

The Slow Fashion Movement is based on the same principles of the Slow Food Movement, as the alternative to mass-produced clothing (AKA "Fast-Fashion"). Initially, The Slow Clothing Movement was intended to reject all mass-produced clothing, referring only to clothing made by hand, but has broadened to include many interpretations and is practiced in various ways.

Some examples of slow fashion practices include:

Opposing and boycotting mass-produced fashion (AKA "Fast-Fashion" or "McFashion").

Choosing artisan products to support smaller businesses, fair trade and locally-made clothes.

Buying secondhand or vintage clothing and donating unwanted garments.

Choosing clothing made with sustainable, ethically-made or recycled fabrics.

Choosing quality garments that will last longer, transcend trends (a "classic" style), and be repairable.

Doing it yourself - making, mending, customizing, altering, and up-cycling your own clothing.

Slowing the rate of fashion consumption: buying fewer clothes less often.

The Slow Fashion movement is a unified representation of all the "sustainable", "eco", "green", and "ethical" fashion movements. It encourages education about the garment industry's connection and impact on the environment and depleting resources, slowing of the supply chain to reduce the number of trends and seasons, to encourage quality production, and return greater value to garments removing the image of disposability of fashion. A key phrase repeatedly heard in reference to Slow Fashion is "quality over quantity". This phrase is used to summarize the basic principles of slowing down the rate of clothing consumption by choosing garments that last longer.

Slow Food

Opposed to the culture of fast food, the sub-movement known as Slow Food seeks to encourage the enjoyment of regional produce, traditional foods, which are often grown organically and to enjoy these foods in the company of others. It aims to defend agricultural biodiversity.

The movement claims 83,000 members in 50 countries, which are organized into 800 Convivia or local chapters. Sometimes operating under a logo of a snail, the collective philosophy is to preserve and support traditional ways of life. Today, 42 states in the U.S. have their own convivium.

In 2004, representatives from food communities in more than 150 countries met in Turin under the umbrella of the Terra Madre (Mother Earth) network.

Slow Gardening

Slow Gardening is a movement that helps gardeners savor what they grow using all their senses through all the seasons. It is not about being lazy; rather it is aimed at getting more out of what they do.

Slow Goods

Slow Goods takes its core direction from various elements of the overall 'Slow Movement' and applying it to the concept, design and manufacturing of physical objects. It focuses on low production runs, the usage of craftspeople within the process and on-shore manufacturing. Proponents

" My doctor told me that I need to slow down, but I don't think I can. "

of this philosophy seek and collaborate with smaller, local supply and service partners.

Slow Goods practitioners must have those tenets baked into their business model, it must be the top driver in the procurement of sustainable materials and manufacturing techniques. The rationale for this local engagement facilitates the assurance of quality, the revitalization of local manufacturing industries and reduces greatly the footprint related to the shipment of goods across regions of land and or water.

This movement seeks to break current conventions of perpetuating the disposable nature of mass production. By using higher quality materials and craftsmanship, items attain a longer lifespan that harkens back to manufacturing golden era of the past.

Slow Media (Slow Television)

Slow Media is a movement aiming at sustainable and focused media production as well as media consumption. It formed in the context of a massive acceleration of news distribution ending in almost real-time digital media such as Twitter.

Followers experiment with a reduction of their daily media intake and log their efforts online ("Slow Media Diet").

Slow Money

Slow Money is a movement to organize investors and donors to steer new sources of capital to small food enterprises, organic farms, and local food systems. Slow Money takes its name from the Slow Food movement. Slow Money aims to develop the relationship between capital markets and place, including social and soil fertility.

Slow Parenting

Slow parenting encourages parents to plan less for their children, instead allowing them to enjoy their childhood and explore the world at their own pace. It is a response to hyper-parenting and 'helicopter' parenting, the widespread trend for parents to schedule activities and classes after school every day and every weekend, to solve problems on behalf of the children, and to buy services from commercial suppliers rather than letting nature take its course.

It was described most specifically by Carl Honoré in Under Pressure: Rescuing Our Children from the Culture Of Hyper-Parenting.

> *Last night we discussed about, that a dog is running from this side to that side. So he's feeling some pleasure. Similarly, we also, so-called civilized man, we are also running on a car, this side and this side. So the same thing -- the dog's race. But we are thinking, because we are running on a car, we are civilized. But the business is that dog's race. So Prahlada Maharaja's point is that we should try to understand the value of life. We should not waste our time by dog's race, either on four legs or on four wheels. That is the point.*
> *~ Srila Prabhupada (Lecture Srimad-Bhagavatam 7.6.3 -- Toronto, June 19, 1976)*

Slow Photography

Slow Photography is a term describing a tendency in today's contemporary Photography and Arts. In response to the spread of digital photography and the snapshot, artists and photographers retake manual techniques and working methods to work slower, manually and in constant dialogue with the physical materials of the images.

Slow Science

The Slow Science movement's objective is to enable scientists to take the time to think and read. The prevalent culture of science is publish or perish, where scientists are judged to be better if they publish more papers in less time, and only these who do so are able to maintain their careers. Those who practice and promote slow science suggest that "society should give scientists the time they need".

"You're telling me it will take 13 years to install my education! What kind of outdated software is this school using?"

Slow Technology

Slow technology approach aims to emphasize that technology can support reflection rather than efficiency. This approach has been discussed through various examples, for example those in interaction design or virtual environments. It is related to other parallel efforts such as those towards reflective design, critical design and critical technical practice.

Slow Travel

Slow Travel is an evolving movement that has taken its inspiration from nineteenth-century European travel writers, such as Théophile Gautier, who reacted against the cult of speed, prompting some modern analysts to ask "If we have slow food and slow cities, then why not slow travel?".

Advocates of slow travel argue that all too often the potential pleasure of the journey is lost by too eager anticipation of arrival. Slow travel, it is asserted, is a state of mind which allows travellers to engage more fully with communities along their route, often favouring visits to spots enjoyed by local residents rather than merely following guidebooks. As such, slow travel shares some common values with ecotourism. Its advocates and devotees generally look for low-impact travel styles, even to the extent of eschewing flying.

Aspects of slow travel, including some of the principles detailed in the Manifesto for Slow Travel, are now increasingly featuring in travel writing. The magazineHidden Europe, which published the Manifesto for Slow Travel, has particularly showcased slow travel, featuring articles that focus on unhurried, low-impact journeys and advocating a stronger engagement with communities that lie en route.

The International Institute of Not Doing Much (IINDM)

The International Institute of Not Doing Much (IINDM) is a humorous approach to the serious topic of time poverty, incivility, and workaholism. The Institute's fictional presence promotes counter-urgency. First created in 2005, SlowDownNow.org is a continually evolving work of art and humor which reports it has over 5,000 members.

References:

The World Institute of Slowness

Wikipedia

Kate Marie & Christopher Thomas (November 10, 2009). Fast Living Slow Ageing. Mileage Media. ISBN 9780980633900.

David Niven Miller. Growth Youthful.

Nunley, Jan (8 January 2008). "Slow Church". anglimergent. 1 March 2013.

Nunley, Jan (4 February 2008), ""Slow Church" Group Page", facebook.com, 1 March 2013

Childress, Kyle (20 May 2008). "Walking with God Slowly". 1 March 2013.

Land, Lucas (11 May 2009). "The Slow Church Movement". 1 March 2013.

Shellnutt, Kate (7 July 2011). "Slow food movement serves as church inspiration". Houston Chronicle. 1 March 2013.

McAteer, Anastasia and John (29 July 2011). "Slow Food, Slow Church". 1 March 2013.

Hauerwas, Stanley (6 July 2012). "Stan and Kyle Talk Slow Church". Slow Church: Abiding Together in the Patient Work of God. Interview with Kyle Childress. Chicago. 2 March 2013.

"Slow Church", facebook.com, 2 March 2013

"Slow Church", Patheos, 1 March 2013

C. Christopher Smith and John Pattison (2014). Slow Church. InterVarsity Press.

Smith, C. Christopher (December 2012). "Slow Down and Know That I Am God: Why it's time for a conversation about Slow Church". Sojourners. 1 March 2013.

Piatt, Christian (7 February 2013). "The Ikea Effect, Slow Church, and Laboring Our Way Into Love". Sojourners. 2 March 2013.

Journal for International Counselor Education 2012 Volume 4, "Slow Counseling: Promoting Wellness in a Fast World"

Fashion: Tailoring a Strategic Approach Towards Sustainability by Maureen Dickson, Carlotta Cataldi, and Crystal Grover

What is Slow Fashion? by Jessica Bourland, Slow Fashioned

Why Giving Up Your Job

Could Be Your Best Career Move Ever!

By Sharon Parsons

A week after leaving the magazine I'd edited for two years, I was phoned by a former colleague bringing what she felt certain was wonderful news.

The top job on a well-respected title was vacant - I should apply, she insisted. 'It's perfect for you,' she said. 'With your experience, you're bound to get it.'

I hesitated, then admitted I'd already been approached. I told her that I wouldn't be going for that editorship, or any other.

There was a stunned silence on the other end of the phone. 'But you can't just quit,' she argued.

Couldn't I? I'd been in magazines all my working life and had always relished the creativity, innovation and buzz. Over the years I'd been promoted, edited a clutch of titles, and enjoyed the rewards. Only a few months previously, I'd been shortlisted for a prestigious award.

But having just celebrated my 50th birthday, something in me had changed. I wasn't only exhausted and disillusioned: I felt permanently stressed and creatively squeezed dry.

Career Woman - The Violence of Modern Jobs And The Lost Art of Home Making

It wasn't just that particular job. It was my whole career as an editor that I found myself questioning. It shocked me to realise that, quite simply, I didn't want to do it any more.

Yet leaving behind my hard-won achievements proved far from easy. In today's competitive, fast-paced society, we're conditioned to believe that people who give up have somehow failed. Onwards and upwards are the only permissible options.

It took a great deal of soul-searching to convince myself that quitting can be the right thing to do — and it was only after I'd come to that lonely and rather shame-faced conclusion that it began to dawn on me that I was part of a growing trend.

I recently wrote a magazine article about learning to love my inner 'quitter', and have been overwhelmed by the number of women who've been in touch to say that they, too, have either thrown in the career towel, or are planning to.

The question is, why? It's not as if it was easy for women of my generation to realise our ambitions.

We 40 and 50-somethings took the beliefs and dreams laid down by the feminists of the 1970s into the workplace and fought hard for recognition, promotion and equal pay.

We have now accepted that we were kidding ourselves to think we could have it all. That's never going to happen while working women still do most of the childcare, organising and housework.

Indeed, a few months ago, Tory MP Louise Mensch resigned her position to devote more time to her children and husband, admitting in a letter to David Cameron: 'I have been unable to make the balancing act work for our family.'

While some applauded her decision, she also attracted howls of protest from others who accused her of letting down the so-called 'sisterhood'.

'It takes a lot of strength and courage to walk away from an established career and the status it brings,' says psychologist Sue Firth. 'Undoubtedly, though, there's some ill-placed guilt around deciding enough is enough.'

She believes we are much more aware that we have choices about the way we live and work today, and feel more empowered to make changes.

'You don't have to stick rigidly to an original career path, no matter what,' she explains. 'Nowadays, it's not unusual to find that the role you took on has changed dramatically, morphing into a position you no longer want.'

'If you're not equipped to take it on, you can feel you're being stretched too thin.'

That was certainly the case for Pree Desai, 33, from Ruislip, North-West London, who returned to her well-paid career as an analyst for an investment bank when her son Anay, now four, was nine months old.

'I'd always loved the buzz of working in such a fast-moving environment,' she said. 'But on the day I went back, Lehman Brothers collapsed — and from then on the pressure was horrendous. Suddenly I was doing the jobs of three people, in a role I barely recognised.'

Although she had supportive colleagues and was allowed to work four days a week, Pree sometimes didn't get home until 11pm, and could go several days without seeing her baby.

By the time she was pregnant with her daughter, Alyssa, now one, Pree had decided she could no longer continue her career. 'It wasn't just because the situation was so stressful,' she says.

'I'd realised how much I was missing by not being at home with Anay, and I didn't want to repeat that.'

Tory MP Louise Mensch resigned her position to devote more time to her children and husband

Luckily her husband, Kish, 32, a City trader, earns a good enough salary to support the family, although Pree misses having her own money to spend.

'I also worry that Kish will think I'm stupid — only able to talk about nappies and feeding,' she admits.

'When he gets home, I want to know every detail about his day. It's a world I'm no longer a part of, but I still take a genuine interest.'

Despite that, Pree has no doubt she did the right thing in walking away. 'When the children are older, 'I'd like to retrain as a financial advisor and work from home,' she says. 'But for now I'm enjoying being a full-time mum.'

One study has found that instead of fretting about what you have to lose by giving up your career, focusing on what you have to gain by walking away makes the process easier.

Sue Firth cautions: 'If you are thinking of quitting — be it for family reasons or because you and your career no longer seem to fit — you must analyse the situation carefully.

'Consider how much you enjoy your job and what, if anything, you'll miss. Talk it through with those you trust: your partner, friends, even a mentor. Most important, before you leave, have a plan in place.'

Mine was to become a writer. But Anna Warrington, 45, took a leap of faith when she resigned from her well-paid position as a facilities manager in the West Midlands four years ago.

'I'd always been very work-orientated — my career defined who I was,' recalls Anna, who was single at the time.

But she had started to feel something was missing. 'I worked long, stressful hours, and I often thought, "Is this it?" she says.

'Then, on holiday in Devon, I made a split-second decision to relocate to the coast. I had no idea what I was going to do, but I was convinced I needed to move.'

Today, Anna is in a relationship with a fisherman and juggles several different jobs, from assisting at a cookery school to cleaning holiday cottages.

'I realised I wasn't bothered by the prestige of a fancy job description, and wanted my life to be more relaxed,' she says. 'Some people are aghast that I've stepped off the career path and think it's a waste, but I couldn't care less.

'I'm proud to say I'm a cleaner, and confident enough not to feel intimidated by high-flyers. I've been there, done that — and I don't need it any more.'

Of course, most of us quitters don't completely abandon the experience we've gained in our careers. Instead we use our existing skills in a different way, as in the case of chartered accountant Susan Stuart, 53, from South London, who is single without children.

Six years ago, she turned her back on the prestigious financial career she'd enjoyed for 30 years.

'I'd always loved my job, but as the working environment became more aggressive, I felt increasingly out of kilter with it,' she explains.

Despite earning a six-figure salary and enjoying an affluent lifestyle, Susan became disillusioned, feeling a growing need to give something back.

'I was on the board of governors at a special needs school while I was still working when I was approached by a charity called Thrive (thrive. org.uk) which aims to change the lives of disabled people through gardening programmes,' she explains.

'I've always been a keen gardener, so it seemed like a great opportunity to satisfy my interest and do something worthwhile.'

She started managing a garden project in Battersea, South London, and is now the charity's interim chief executive.

Susan loves the direction her new career has taken. 'It's fantastic to use my skills — from team-building to project funding — to help develop the charity,' she says.

'What's so rewarding is seeing tangible results, and building strong, durable relationships — something that no longer happened in my previous job.

'I don't earn anything like what I did before, but I'm so much happier.'

And me? When I walked away from my career, a friend gave me the classic self-help book by Susan Jeffers, Feel The Fear and Do It Anyway.

I'm embarrassed to say that it's still languishing, unread, on the bookshelf. I'd felt the fear, I'd done it anyway — and I've never looked back.

Source:
Sharon Parsons, The Daily Mail, 7 October 2012

> *Therefore sastra says, nayam deho deha-bhajam nrloke kastan kaman arhate vid-bhujam ye [SB 5.5.1]. This was the instruction given by King Rsabhadeva, whose son's name was Maharaja Bharata, under whose name this land, this planet is called Bharatavarsa. So He instructed His sons, "My dear sons, don't spoil your life simply working hard for sense gratification like the hogs. Because the hog is also working day and night, but what is the aim? The aim is sense gratification. At night sleep or have sex life, and at daytime collect money and spend it for family maintenance or some sense gratification. This is not meant for human life." Now, this morning one gentleman was asking us that we are not working. We are not working. They think... He is a lawyer. He thinks that unless one works very hard for sense gratification, he is not human being or he is not doing his duty perfectly. That is his idea. But actual life is to become perfect, from the platform of animal life come to the perfection of life. Therefore Krsna says, manusyanam sahasresu [Bg. 7.3]. Everyone is thinking that "Work very hard like the hogs and dogs, and find out your means of sense enjoyment, and then enjoy it." This is called karmi life. They have no other idea. You will find everyone is working hard. From morning at six o'clock till ten o'clock at night they're working hard. What is the purpose? To get some money and utilize it for sense gratification. This is animal life; this is not human life. But they are thinking that one who does not work so hard day and night for sense gratification, he is not doing. He is escaping.*
>
> ~ Srila Prabhupada (Bhagavad-gita 7.3 -- London, March 11, 1975)

28

A Family Of Four With No Jobs

Self-Sufficient In The City

Three Tons Of Food Per Year From A 1/10 Acre City Lot

Jules Dervaes is an urban farmer and a proponent of the urban homesteading movement. Dervaes and his three adult children operate an urban market garden in Pasadena, California as well as other websites and online stores related to self-sufficiency and "adapting in place." This is a family of four with no jobs and a beautiful life.

Dervaes has a one-tenth acre lot in Pasadena, California, on which he and his family raise three tons of food per year. This provides 75 percent of their annual food needs and helps them sustain an organic produce business. They also raise bees and compost worms.

Dervaes started experimenting with self-sufficiency while he lived in New Zealand and later in Florida, then decided to see how efficient he could make an urban homestead in Pasadena, California, USA.

According to Natural Home magazine, *"The Dervaeses' operation is about 60 to 150 times as efficient as their industrial competitors, without relying on chemical fertilizers and pesticides."*

In addition to growing a significant amount of food, the Derveas family attempts to live off-grid as far as possible and have invested significant amounts of money to experiment with other ways of attaining self-sufficiency. They have 12 solar panels on the  roof of the house, a biodiesel filling station in the garage, and a solar oven in the backyard; they use a wastewater reclamation system, a dual-flush toilet, a composting toilet, and a number of hand-cranked kitchen appliances (to reduce power consumption). They also use solar drying, and have a cob oven.

Dervaes owns several websites, including julesdervaes.com, pathtofreedom.com, urbanhomestead.org, urbanhomesteading.com, freedomgardens.org, peddlrswagon.com, backyardchickens.org, barnyardsandbackyards.org, thehiddenyears.org, and dervaesinstitute.org. As of 2008, Path to Freedom got five million hits per month from over 125 different countries.

> *The gigantic industrial enterprises are products of a godless civilization. Godless civilization, they no more can depend on the natural gifts. They think by industrial enterprises, they will get more money and they'll be happy. And to remain satisfied with the food grains, vegetables and natural gifts, that is primitive idea. They say, "It is primitive." When men were not civilized, they would depend on nature, but when they are advanced in civilization, they must discover industrial enterprises.*
>
> *They do not know what is spiritual life, what is ultimate goal. Simply like cats and dogs. The dog jumps over with four legs, and if a man can jump over with four wheels, then that is advancement. Just see.*
>
> *~ Srila Prabhupada (Lecture, Srimad-Bhagavatam, Mayapura, October 20, 1974)*

The Dervaes family was featured on National Geographic Channel's Doomsday Preppers in 2012 and briefly appeared in a trailer for the show.

29

Need For A Social Structure

This exchange between His Divine Grace A.C. Bhaktivedanta Swami Prabhupada and Australia's director of research for the Department of Social Welfare took place at the Melbourne ISKCON center, on May 21, 1975.

Srila Prabhupada: The defect of the Western countries is that practically there is no social structure. The father and mother divorce, and the children become aimless. In most cases this is the defect.

Director: That happens. Yes.

Srila Prabhupada: I have seen this pattern with many of my students. Their whole family becomes disrupted, because the father and mother -- even in old age -- divorce. I have seen the mother of one of my students. His father was a very good businessman. Very nice family, with a good income. All of a sudden, the father and mother disagreed about something and got a divorce. The sons were thrown into confusion; the daughters were thrown into confusion.

Director: That's the kind of cases we deal with.

Srila Prabhupada: The father married again, and the mother married again. They were not happy, and also, the business closed. So by this one instance I can understand how, in the Western countries, people have broken away from the traditional social structure. Of course, the root cause is godlessness. That is the root cause.

Director: And now divorce is getting easier, too. Isn't it?

Srila Prabhupada: That is a very dangerous law -- to allow divorce. Divorce should not be allowed. Even if there is some disagreement between husband and wife, it should be ignored. The great political strategist Canakya Pandita says, dampatye kalahe caiva bahvarambhe laghu kriya: "The husband and wife's quarrel should not be taken very seriously." Further, aja yuddhe: "A marital fight is just like a fight between two goats." The goats may be fighting very spiritedly, but if you say "Hut!" they will go away. Similarly, the fight between husband and wife should not be taken very seriously. Let them fight for some time; they will stop automatically. But now when the husband and wife fight, each goes to a lawyer, and the lawyers give encouragement. "Yes, let us go to the divorce court." This is going on.

So the first defect of modern society is the law allowing divorce. Another defect: there is no method for training a man to become first-class. That method is there in the Vedic civilization. Now, of course, that method is also abolished, due to the degradation of this modern age.

Formerly, though, society was divided into four classes -- brahmanas, ksatriyas, vaisyas, sudras: advisors, administrators, merchants, and workers. The brahmanas were first-class men -- ideal. But in today's society there is no ideal man. Society should have some living example, so that people can see, "Oh, here is an ideal man." And the ideal man is described here in our Bhagavad-gita. Any man can be trained. And if even just one percent of the people become ideal, the remaining ninety-nine percent will see and follow. But now there are no ideal men. That is the defect.

So we are training people to become ideal men. That is the purpose of this movement. And in practical terms, you can see what our students were in their previous life and what they are now. Therefore, the government should establish an institution to create ideal men. We can help.

But now there is no such facility. We are training our students, but sometimes people laugh: "What is this nonsense?" They criticize.

Career Woman - The Violence of Modern Jobs And The Lost Art of Home Making

These leaders of society do not encourage us. Yesterday I was talking with a priest, and about illicit sex he said, "What is the wrong there? It is a great pleasure."

We are training our students according to actual spiritual principles, and so we are proclaiming that illicit sex is sinful. In fact, our first condition is that one must give up these four things: illicit sex, meat-eating, intoxication, and gambling. This is my first condition before accepting people as my students. So they agree and they follow.

At least, formerly in India there was no drinking propaganda. Now the government is even making that. They are opening wine shops. In India, even in the British period, drinking was very, very restricted. Very, very restricted. First of all, in Indian society if anyone drank, he was rejected; he was not regarded as a gentleman. A drunkard was never respected.

"I use to lose my secretaries because they were getting married - now they leave to start their own companies."

Similarly, meat-eaters. A meat-eater was considered a third-class man. In our childhood we saw that when people learned to eat meat, they did it very secretly, not within their own home. Instead, they ate meat far away from home, with someone else doing the cooking. It was considered very abominable to eat meat or to drink.

As for illicit sex, that also was very rare. Young women were kept strictly under the supervision of parents. The father would see that his daughter did not mix with any boy. If a girl were to go out at night and not come back, then her life would be finished -- nobody would marry her. So the father had to keep his daughter with great care. And he was very, very anxious to find a suitable boy to whom he could hand his daughter over for marriage. We saw all this in our childhood. But now these nice social customs are slackened. Jawaharlal Nehru, our late prime minister, introduced the divorce law, and now Indian society is in a chaotic condition.

Director: What can you do if society wants divorce? Society wants it that way.

Srila Prabhupada: "Society wants it." That's like your child wants to go to hell -- but it is not your duty as his father to allow him to go to hell.

"Society wants it." Society does not know the proper standard of spiritual behavior, nor does the government know how to uplift people. The government does not know. For all the government knows, the animals and we human beings are the same. Simply, the animals loiter naked, and we are nicely dressed -- that's all. Civilization finished. I remain an animal, but my advancement is that I am very nicely dressed. That is the standard now.

But our Vedic civilization is not like that. The two-legged animal must change his consciousness. He must be trained up as a human being.

[To a disciple:] Bhagavad-gita lists the qualities of the first-class man. You can read them.

Disciple: Samo damas tapah saucam ksantir arjavam eva ca / jnanam vijnanam astikyam brahma-karma svabhava-jam: "Peacefulness, self-control, austerity, purity, tolerance, honesty, knowledge, wisdom, and religiousness -- these are the natural qualities by which the brahmanas work."

Srila Prabhupada: So people should be trained according to these spiritual principles. If there is no training, how can you expect nice citizens? If you allow a child to smoke from the very beginning and to commit all kinds of other sinful activities, how can you expect him to be a nice gentleman when he is grown up? It is not possible.

Creating ideal men is possible through this Krsna consciousness movement. It is not that all men can be trained up spiritually. But if even a small percentage of ideal men are in society, at least people will think, "Oh, here is the ideal."

THE AUTHOR

Dr. Sahadeva dasa (Sanjay Shah) is a monk in vaisnava tradition. His areas of work include research in Vedic and contemporary thought, corporate and educational training, social work and counselling, travelling, writing books and of course, practicing spiritual life and spreading awareness about the same.

He is also an accomplished musician, composer, singer, instruments player and sound engineer. He has more than a dozen albums to his credit so far. (SoulMelodies.com)

His varied interests include alternative holistic living, Vedic studies, social criticism, environment, linguistics, history, art & crafts, nature studies, web technologies etc.

Many of his books have been acclaimed internationally and translated in other languages.

By The Same Author

Oil-Final Countdown To A Global Crisis And Its Solutions
End of Modern Civilization And Alternative Future
To Kill Cow Means To End Human Civilization
Cow And Humanity - Made For Each Other
Cows Are Cool - Love 'Em!
Let's Be Friends - A Curious, Calm Cow
Wondrous Glories of Vraja
We Feel Just Like You Do
Tsunami Of Diseases Headed Our Way - Know Your Food Before Time Runs Out
Cow Killing And Beef Export - The Master Plan To Turn India Into A Desert
Capitalism Communism And Cowism - A New Economics For The 21st Century
Noble Cow - Munching Grass, Looking Curious And Just Hanging Around
World - Through The Eyes Of Scriptures
To Save Time Is To Lengthen Life
Life Is Nothing But Time - Time Is Life, Life Is Time
Lost Time Is Never Found Again
Spare Us Some Carcasses - An Appeal From The Vultures
An Inch of Time Can Not Be Bought With A Mile of Gold
Cow Dung For Food Security And Survival of Human Race
Cow Dung – A Down To Earth Solution To Global Warming And Climate Change
Corporatocracy - You Are A Corporate Citizen, A Slave of Invisible And Ruthless Masters
Working Moms And The Rise of A Lost Generation
Glories of Thy Wondrous Name
India A World Leader in Cow Killing And Beef Export - An Italian Did It In 10 Years
As Long As There Are Slaughterhouses, There Will Be Wars
Peak Soil – Industrial Civilization, On The Verge of Eating Itself
If Violence Has To Stop, Slaughterhouses Must Close Down
(More information on availability on DrDasa.com)

www.ingramcontent.com/pod-product-compliance
Lightning Source LLC
Chambersburg PA
CBHW061322040426
42444CB00011B/2730